Know Your Rights
Employment and Family Rights

'Andrew McCann's *Know Your Rights: Employment and Family Rights* is a most helpful and practical aid to the ordinary citizen in dealing with situations that may arise in the areas of employment and relationships within the family. It is written in an easy and accessible style and will be very useful to people dealing with difficult situations. It asks the kind of questions the average citizen confronted with a problematic situation would like to have answered and answers them well, simply and practically but with a clear and extensive knowledge of the legal and political background required to give such answers.'

Senator David Norris

'Andrew's advice is always relevant, and presented in a way which is easy to understand. Whenever we announce he is coming on to the *Shaun Doherty Show*, the phone lines light up immediately, and queries start coming in via text and e-mail. There are many people out there in need of advice they can trust, and they know that's what they'll get from Andrew McCann.'

Shaun Doherty, presenter of the Shaun Doherty Show, *Highland Radio*

'More and more, we need to know our rights and our entitlements in society. This book is a great addition to the library of the concerned and involved citizen.'

Joe Duffy, presenter of Liveline, *RTÉ Radio 1*

Know Your Rights

Employment and Family Rights

Andrew McCann

ORPEN PRESS

6053954

Published by
Orpen Press
Lonsdale House
Avoca Avenue
Blackrock
Co. Dublin
Ireland

e-mail: info@orpenpress.com
www.orpenpress.com

ISBN 978-1-871305-77-7

Printed in Ireland by Colorman Ltd

About the Author

Andrew McCann is the author, since 2006, of the annual publication *Know Your Rights* (Orpen Press), now in its seventh edition, and is a consumer advocate since 2002.

Andrew is a regular contributor to TV (TV3 – *Ireland AM*, weekdays 7 a.m.–10 a.m.) since 2006, national radio (2FM – *Colm Hayes Show*, weekdays 11 a.m.–1 p.m. and previously on the *Gerry Ryan Show*; Newstalk – *Lunchtime with Jonathan Healy*, weekdays 12 p.m.–1.30 p.m.), regional radio (Highland Radio in Donegal) and local radio.

Andrew has also published articles on consumer rights in national newspapers (*Irish Examiner* and *The Sun*) and in magazines (*You & Your Money*).

Andrew McCann holds a bachelor of arts in Law (Dublin Institute of Technology) and is a graduate of the Marketing Institute of Ireland. He has also successfully completed a higher certificate in Advocacy (Sligo Institute of Technology) and has a certificate in Management Skills for Managers of Advocacy Services (Institute of Technology, Blanchardstown). He has also completed a diploma in Social Studies and accredited training in the area of mediation.

Previously, Andrew worked as a management consult-
ant in the area of customer relationship management and
for a large telecoms company in various roles.

Andrew is married and lives in Kinsealy, Malahide, Co.
Dublin.

Contents

Contents

Contents

Disclaimer and Waiver of Liability

Whilst every effort has been made to ensure the accuracy of the information and material contained in this book, nevertheless it is possible that errors or omissions may occur in the content. The author and publishers assume no responsibility for and give no guarantees or warranties concerning the accuracy, completeness or up-to-date nature of the information provided in this book. The author and publishers do not accept any liability for the consequences of any actions taken, legal or otherwise, on the basis of the information provided in this book. This book is not a complete source of information on all aspects of social and civic rights. If you need professional or legal advice you should consult a suitably qualified person.

Introduction

The idea for *Know Your Rights: Employment and Family Rights* came from a broad spectrum of directions, especially legislative changes in the last two years and changes in the employment landscape.

In the last two years I have seen a vast increase in complaints in relation to employment disputes, specifically in relation to redundancies, selection for redundancy, unfair dismissals and outstanding payments due to employees linked to the liquidation and closure of businesses.

In 2011, 9,206 referrals (which contained multiple complaints) were made to the Rights Commissioner Service, with the largest sector being breaches of the Payment of Wages Act (non-payment or unlawful deductions of pay). In the period 2007–2011 there were 58,000 referrals to the Rights Commissioner Service (*Labour Relations Commission Annual Report 2011*). As well as this, 8,458 cases were referred to the Employment Appeals Tribunal in 2011, although only 6,723 were dealt with in 2011. The waiting periods for cases to be heard was between 76 and 77 weeks in 2011 (*Employment Appeals Tribunal Annual Report 2011*).

I have also seen increased tensions between employers and employees due to the current economic downturn and the indirect impact of forced changes within the workplace to adapt to the new circumstances.

In 2012 we have also seen the commencement of a new method of employment redress with the commencement of a new centralised single complaint form through www. workplacerelations.ie for all employment and employment equality cases. This will be followed by reform of the complaints bodies and a more simplified redress system with the passing of the newly proposed Workplace Relations Bill in 2013.

We have also seen the introduction of new legislation for agency workers transposing EU legislation to provide equal treatment to agency workers compared to regular workers. This is the final part of the jigsaw which also has previously seen the passing of legislation in the past decade to provide protection to both part-time and fixed-term workers comparable to regular workers.

Finally, we have also seen new legislation in the industrial relations area as a direct consequence of a court challenge in 2011 in relation to EROs (Employment Regulation Orders) and REAs (Registered Employment Agreements) and the reversal of the minimum wage back to €8.65 per hour (from the previously reduced rate of €7.65 per hour implemented in 2010).

In the family law area the biggest change has been the implementation of the Civil Partnership and Certain Rights and Obligations of Cohabitants Act 2010, which had full effect in 2011. There were 4,042 same-sex couples living together in 2011, of which 2,321 (57.4 per cent) were male and 1,721 (42.6 per cent) were female. This new legislation provides equal treatment to registered civil partners compared to married couples as well as imposing certain rights and obligations on cohabitants to each other if the relationship ends. This, of course, is subject to a number of eligibility criteria, including the length of the relationship and whether or not the couple have children. This is a fundamental change in legislation not just for civil partners but also for cohabitants. The impact of this legislation is far-reaching and many couples (same or opposite sex) are not aware of the implications and will be surprised when reading the possible consequences in this book.

We have seen the passing of the Children's Referendum in November 2012, which will have far-reaching effects in relation to future adoption of children and the responsibility of the State and its citizens. We have also seen the High Court challenge of the McCann case (2009) and the impact this has had on maintenance debt, which in turn led to the passing of the Civil Law (Miscellaneous Provisions) Act 2011 to amend procedures in relation to maintenance debt.

Recent results from Census 2011 show that the number of divorces has increased by 150 per cent to over 87,000 since 2002, while the number of separated couples has increased and levelled off at over 116,000 from 107,000 in 2006. In addition, the rate of marriage has been declining slightly since 2007. In 2011 there were 19,879 marriages, compared to 22,756 in 2007.

Chapter 1 examines the key differences between employees and self-employment in employment law and why it is important to make the distinction. In this chapter we also examine the importance and requirements of the provision of terms and conditions of employment. We discuss the vast area of pay cuts, and redundancy and unfair dismissal, and the key differences between both. In this chapter we also discuss the area of breaks, public holiday entitlements, annual leave entitlements, sick pay and

Sunday working. Finally, we discuss the delicate area of discrimination, stress, bullying and harassment.

Chapter 2 examines additional employment rights covering a vast area such as maternity, paternity, parental, compassionate and carer's leave. We then examine the protection of both part-time and fixed-term workers compared to their regular permanent colleagues. Finally, we talk about the whole dispute resolution process, the existing requirements and timeframes for complaints, how to make a complaint and the proposed restructuring of the redress bodies and system with the Workplace Relations Bill.

Chapter 3 examines the areas of guardianship, access, custody and adoption. We also discuss in detail maintenance and the new obligations of former cohabitants to pay maintenance not just for their children but also possibly for former cohabitants. We discuss the difficult area of domestic violence and the new range of options to redress the situation. Finally, we discuss wills and inheritance, the importance of making a will, the new rights for registered civil partners and complications that may arise in administering probate.

Chapter 4 looks at the area of marriage and civil partnership and the legal pre-requisites. We also examine prenuptials and mediation. Marriage and relationship breakdown is a large subject, and we examine in detail separation, judicial separation, nullity, dissolution of civil partnership and divorce, and the implications for both married and civil partners and former cohabiting couples. Finally, we examine eligibility for legal aid and the protection of the family home.

Know Your Rights: Employment and Family Rights answers a vast range of topical day-to-day questions relevant to the consumer and citizen. If you have a question that has not been covered in this book, please send it in and I will do my best to address it. Questions should be forwarded to:

Orpen Press
Lonsdale House
Avoca Avenue
Blackrock
Co. Dublin
Tel: 01 2785090
E-mail: info@orpenpress.com

I can also be contacted through my website: www. yourrights.ie.

CHAPTER 1

Introduction to Employment Rights

Employees and Employers

A month ago I started doing some work for a large telecoms company. They provided the work and I provided the van. When I enquired about my pay, they told me I would have to forward an invoice. I am now told I will not receive the same holiday entitlements as the other employees. What should I do? I thought I was an employee.

Before examining holiday entitlements, we must determine if this person is an employee or self-employed. This is essential, as only employees are protected and have the right to paid leave under employment legislation. Therefore we must distinguish between a 'contract of employment', which sets out the employer–employee relationship, and a 'contract for service', which is a contract between a business or agency and a self-employed person. So, who is an employee? An employee is a person who works under a contract of employment for another person, known as the employer. Under this contract, the employer has the right to direct the employee, not only as to what has to be done, but also as to how it is to be done.

Therefore it is important to determine all the facts, as your status as an employee or not will have major implications for your working conditions, insurance liability, payment implications, disputes and leave.

The other main differences between being an employee and being self-employed relate to taxation and social welfare classification. With reference to taxation, who is responsible for administering your tax affairs? As a PAYE (Pay As You Earn) worker, the employer is responsible for your tax returns, payslips, P60 and P45, if required. If you are self-employed, you must register with Revenue, complete self-assessment tax returns yearly, and register for VAT and public liability insurance (if applicable).

Regarding social welfare classification, it is important to distinguish which category of contribution you pay and what benefits are applicable (short- and long-term). The essential distinction is between Class A (PAYE worker) and Class S (self-employed).

How can you determine if someone is self-employed or an employee?

There are a number of different tests that determine this:

- The Control Test determines who controls the relationship between the parties, i.e. when, where and how the work is carried out.
- The Integration Test determines if the person is an integral part of the organisation, i.e. if the person appears to be part of the workforce or if they are treated separately to other employees in carrying out their duties.
- The Enterprise Test determines if the person has invested their own capital and equipment, and if there is an element of risk involved.

- The Mixed Test reviews all of the above factors (control, integration and enterprise). Essentially, the Mixed Test looks at the balance of probabilities and the practicalities of assessing the situation in each case.

Other factors that differentiate the employee from one who is self-employed are:

- Employment and dismissal – who does the hiring and firing, and by what method?
- Times of work and workplace – the greater the flexibility in relation to start and finish times, and location of work completed, the higher the probability of self-employment.
- Equipment – the greater the capital input, i.e. money or equipment invested, the higher the probability of self-employment.

To determine your status if you have not yet started work or haven't yet been paid, the following may apply:

- Your case may have to be assessed by the Employment Appeals Tribunal (EAT) to determine your classification. (See also Code of Practice for Determining Employment or Self-Employment Status of Individuals – revised June 2010.) The code is available from www.workplace relations.ie.
- Also, you may have to get in contact with the Scope Section of the Department of Social Protection to determine your PRSI classification.

Does it really make a difference what PRSI classification I am?

Yes, your classification will determine whether or not you

3

are protected under employment legislation and to what extent you are covered for social welfare payments. Your classification will also determine what tax administration system you must comply with, i.e. Self-Assessment (yearly tax returns to Revenue) or PAYE (tax deducted at source in your payroll). Your classification will also determine if you require insurance indemnity (protection for personal injury, professional indemnity (quality of workmanship) or third-party damage). You will also need to consider the relevant dispute resolution mechanism. If you are an employee, your contract and terms and conditions are your fundamental protections, in conjunction with employment legislation. If you are self-employed, legal contractual agreements must be in place regarding disputes, provision of certain levels of service, and termination of contracts. Breaches of such contracts may only be adjudicated through agreed or legal recourse.

I am an agency worker (nurse) and have worked in the same location now for over six months. Who is my employer?
In general, the employer is the body that pays your wage. Therefore, if you are paid by the agency, the agency is your employer (and is liable for your PRSI). This may also be applicable if you become pregnant and seek leave under the Maternity Protection Acts 1994 and 2004. However, although you are being paid by the agency, your place of employment is liable for all your health and safety requirements and any possible case in relation to unfair dismissal (if applicable), subject to normal criteria.

The European Temporary Agency Directive (which was adopted in June 2008 and came into full effect on 5 December 2011) now also imposes equal treatment (from day one) for all agency workers (section 6), compared to other employees (including pay, working conditions and employment equality), as well as equal access to training, childcare, canteen facilities, parking (section 14) and permanent employment opportunities (section 11). This also compels the employer ("hirer") to inform the agency of the facilities available (section 15). The right to equal pay has full backdated effect since 5 December 2011.

It will also be an offence for an employment agency to charge a fee to facilitate an agency worker to commence direct employment with their prospective employer, i.e. the employer where they are located or in legislation known as "the hirer" (section 13).

The EU Directive was imposed into Irish law on 16 May 2012 under the Protection of Employees (Temporary Agency Work) Act 2012.

The Employment Agency Regulation Bill 2009 proposes to regulate the employment agency sector by the establishment of a statutory code of practice that would set out standards (section 27), impose a requirement to have a licence (granted and approved by the Minister for Jobs, Enterprise and Innovation) (section 10), protect whistleblowers (section 29), prosecute employment agencies from outside Ireland that fail to appear in court for offences in employment legislation (section 26) and establish a Monitoring and Advisory Committee (section 33).

So who is an agency worker?
Under the Protection of Employees (Temporary Agency Work) Act 2012 an agency worker is defined as "an individual employed by an employment agency under a contract of employment by virtue of which the individual may be assigned to work for, and under the direction and supervision of, a person other than an

employment agency." The Act does not apply to persons training or participating in an approved course under a FAS programme or other publicly funded Government programmes.

What happens to my pay if I am between jobs with the agency?
Section 6(2) of the Protection of Employees (Temporary Agency Work) Act 2012 states that before an agency worker enters into a contract with an agency they must be advised in writing that their pay between assignments (jobs) may not be less than half their normal rate of pay (i.e. the rate they would have received in their last assignment), subject to not being paid lower than the national minimum wage. Section 7 states that for clarity purposes, gaps between assignments (jobs) for the assessment of continuous rates must be greater than three months (section 7). Collective agreements may be in place with the Labour Court (subject to its approval) allowing variation on the rates, compared to permanent employees (section 8).

Will I be protected as a "whistleblower" if I make a complaint?
Yes, under the Act an agency worker will be protected (sections 21–24) from making a complaint as long as the complaint is made in good faith, and is not a knowingly false statement. In addition, the employer/hirer cannot punish you for validly setting down a complaint. Protection will be removed in cases where the statement was made knowing it to be false, and fines or imprisonment can be imposed in those cases.

SUMMARY CHECKLIST: Employees and Employers

Are you an employee or self-employed? ☐
What is the relationship between the parties? Do you have ☐ a 'contract of employment' with terms and conditions, or do you have a 'contract for service'?
How has your payment been administered, i.e. pay packet ☐ with deductions, or invoices?
Do you have to use the Integration, Control, Enterprise or ☐ Mixed Tests to assess your status?
Have you commenced employment yet and, if so, what clas- ☐ sification of PRSI contribution do you pay?
Does your case need to be investigated by the Scope ☐ Section of the Department of Social Protection or by the Employment Appeals Tribunal for clarification?
If you are an agency worker, who pays you, and who is ☐ responsible for your employment rights?

Terms of Employment

When should I receive a copy of my terms and conditions of employment?
You should receive a copy of your terms and conditions of employment within two months of the date of commencement of employment or, for employees who began their employment prior to May 1994, within two months upon request. All employees, regardless of hours worked, must receive a contract of employment.

We normally have an afternoon break from work, but our contract doesn't specifically state this. Is this agreement officially in place?
In reviewing the answer, we need to look at all the terms (express and implied) of employment. Express terms are

7

terms that are specifically stated in the contract of employment. Implied terms are terms that are implied through common agreements or by legislation, which are not specifically set down in writing, e.g. the employer will provide a safe place of work for the employee.

An employer cannot state express terms that are in breach of specific terms of legislation, e.g. minimum terms of notice, etc. An employer may set down express terms in excess of the minimum requirements in the contract, e.g. one month's notice required by the employer from the employee, if the latter is leaving the job.

Specific requirements have been established in drafting terms of employment, laid down by the Terms of Employment (Information) Act 1994–2001. This Act specifies that the contract must be in writing and include the following:

- Names of employer and employee
- Addresses of employer and employee
- Place of work
- Job description and/or job title
- A clause stating that the employee is bound to obey all reasonable requests
- Date of commencement of employment
- Rate of pay, amount and method of calculation, and pension entitlements (if applicable)
- Hours of work (including overtime rate when applicable)
- Entitlement to paid leave and sick pay (if any)
- Notice periods and rest breaks
- Any collective agreements in existence, i.e. agreements of specific arrangements for employees in specific sectors, such as trade groups, and their respective agreed

terms either under a registered Employment Regulation Order (ERO) or Registered Employment Agreement (REA)
- Details of employment outside the State (if applicable)
- The governing jurisdiction of employment legislation, e.g. Irish or UK law (subject to where you pay your PRSI contributions), and/or if employment will occur outside the agreed jurisdiction (if greater than one month)
- Status of employment, i.e. fixed-term, fixed-purpose, permanent, etc.

There are additional express terms which, although not compulsory, are advisable:

- Probationary period
- Details of travel and subsistence
- Health and safety regulations and requirements
- Applicable trade union association
- Retirement age (if applicable)
- Disciplinary and grievance procedure
- Harassment or sexual harassment and bullying policy

There are four main types of terms implied in the employment contract:

- Terms implied from custom and practice, or terms implied in fact – these become incorporated due to continuous long-term use and practice, e.g. half an hour off work to cash cheques (before the implementation of electronic banking).
- Terms implied by common law – such terms can refer to both the employer's and employee's duties.

Employer's Duties	Employee's Duties
Duty to pay	Duty to use due care and skill regarding employer's property and other employees
Duty to take reasonable care for the safety of the employee	Duty to obey all reasonable orders of employers
Duty to act fairly	General duty not to damage employer's business and reputation
Implied duty of trust	Implied duty not to disclose trade secrets after leaving employment

- Terms implied by statute – legislation protecting employment rights
- Terms implied by collective agreements – these are collective agreements between trade unions and employers' bodies. The new Industrial Relations (Amendment) Act 2012 provides a new framework for the establishment and review of Joint Labour Committees (JLCs) and registered Employment Regulation Orders (EROs) (discussed later).

Therefore, in summary, if the practice of afternoon breaks has been in operation as a recognised custom and practice, and has been accepted by both the employer and employees, it may be reasonable to continue the practice. It is important to consider that if any alternative new arrangement has been developed or agreed between the parties, either through collective agreements or through new working practices discussed and approved in consultation with employees, the previous custom and practice may therefore be removed in time.

So what happened in July 2011 in relation to Employment Regulation Orders (EROs) set down by the Joint Labour Committees (JLCs)? Someone said they were abolished. Is this true?

Yes, Mr Justice Feeney stated on 7 July 2011 that all EROs from that date forward were invalid and had no further statutory effect.

EROs were agreements in place in certain sectors of employment that set down minimum statutory entitlements for employees in relation to pay, overtime and premium payments. Generally, these rates were over and above the minimum entitlements. The sectors affected were:

- Aerated waters and wholesale bottling
- Agricultural workers
- Brush and broom
- Catering (Dublin and Dun Laoghaire)
- Catering (other)
- Contract cleaning (Dublin)
- Contract cleaning (other)
- Hairdressing (Cork)
- Hairdressing (Dublin, Dun Laoghaire and Bray)
- Handkerchief and household piece goods
- Hotels (Dublin and Dun Laoghaire)
- Hotels (other excluding Cork)
- Law clerks
- Provender milling
- Retail, grocery and allied trades
- Security industry
- Shirt making
- Tailoring
- Women's clothing and millinery

What this means in a practical sense is that all employees (from this date forward) are entitled under law to receive the minimum entitlements under law, and for employers it also means that they too must comply with existing employment legislation requirements. Further details can be found on www.labourcourt.ie.

What if I was employed under an ERO prior to 7 July 2011. Should my pay be reduced?
As you are an existing employee, with existing terms and conditions of employment, it could be argued that any reduction in pay is in breach of your terms and conditions of employment, and therefore any changes to your terms and conditions of employment cannot be imposed without prior agreement or by legislation (discussed below).

Were Registered Employment Agreements (REAs) affected by this change?
No, REAs or collective agreements were not affected by this change. REAs are agreements between employers' and employees' bodies registered with the Labour Court. REAs are present in the following trades:

- Drapery, footwear and allied trades (Dublin and Dun Laoghaire)
- Construction industry
- Printing (Dublin)
- Electrical contracting
- Contract cleaning
- Overhead powerline contractors

Further details can be found on www.labourcourt.ie.

So has any legislation been passed to re-regulate the situation in relation to REAs?

Yes, the Industrial Relations (Amendment) Act 2012 has since been passed. The purpose of the Act is to provide better working relations between workers and employers. From now on (section 5) all new applications for a Registered Employment Agreement must send a copy of the agreement and agreement from the parties to the Labour Court. The Labour Court may decline the application if there is a belief the parties (to the agreement) are not substantially representative of the workers, taking into account the number of workers represented by the union and the total number of workers overall in the sector, and also if there is any question of doubt that the agreement will not improve working relationships. If approved, the agreement will be binding on all employees. Upon approval, a copy of the agreement will be forwarded to the Minister for Jobs, Enterprise and Innovation for final approval.

If either party to the agreement (employer or employee) wishes to vary a term in the agreement, this can be done by mutual agreement (section 6(28)(2)). If agreement between the parties cannot be reached, the existing dispute mechanisms, i.e. Labour Relations Commission, can be utilised. Employers may propose a variation in the Registered Employment Agreement on economic grounds (only after twelve months from its registration or last variation), and, if approved, this can be implemented. Section 7 of the Act now grants the Labour Court authority to review REAs upon the written request of an interested party or the Minister for Jobs, Enterprise and Innovation and it has the power to cancel the REA if satisfied there has been a substantial change in circumstances of the trade or business or if there is no longer substantial representation of the workers.

If the employer fails to follow the order of the Minister to comply with the REA within 28 days of the date of the order, workers, a trade union or the Minister for Jobs, Enterprise and Innovation may apply to the Circuit Court to impose an order (without the need to present the facts). The Court has the power to impose interest on the payment due.

Employers may submit an application to seek an exemption from payment of the REA on economic grounds (under section 9). If approved, the exemption may last for up to 24 months. Exemptions will not be granted if one was previously granted within the last five years. In seeking an exemption a tax clearance certificate and supporting information (financial and otherwise) must be provided. In addition, an agreement must also be in place with the majority of workers, and/or the majority of representatives. Any reduction must not be below the national minimum wage or reduce pension contributions paid by the employer on behalf of the workers.

How have EROs been affected by the change in legislation?
The new legislation now imposes an extensive review, at least every five years, of each Joint Labour Committee, including submissions, representations and membership (section 11). The review may recommend continuing, amalgamating or abolishing the JLC. In addition, proposals may include fixing the minimum rates of pay and regulating conditions of employment (section 12). All factors will be considered upon developing proposals, including the financial viability or otherwise of the ERO and maintaining sustainable working relationships.

Employment Regulation Orders must be approved by the Labour Court and forwarded to the Minister for Jobs, Enterprise and Innovation for approval.

Upon approval, a worker, trade union or the Minister can submit a complaint to the Rights Commissioner if there is a breach of the ERO, and the maximum award payable is up to two years' pay (section 13(3)). All complaints must be made within six months of the date the ERO was first breached. A right of appeal will be available to either party. If the employer fails to carry out the decision of the Rights Commissioner an enforcement order can be brought before the Labour Court (without a need to hear the case). In the case of a "winding up" or bankruptcy, payments due under the breach will be classed as a priority (section 45D). There may be an exemption granted to an employer from paying the statutory minimum pay (section 14) subject to the same procedure laid out in relation to REAs above.

I don't know all my employment rights. Should my rights not be easily available and displayed visibly in my workplace?

In the proposed Employment Law Compliance Bill 2008, employers will be obliged to display information about employment legislation in the workplace, and this information must be in a prominent place and in an understandable language or languages. The information must also include complaints procedures and relevant complaints bodies, as well as the contact details of the National Employment Rights Authority (NERA) (www. employmentrights.ie). There has been no progress with this Bill since the dissolution of the last Government on 1 February 2011.

In addition, there is proposed further reform under the Workplace Relations (Law Reform) Bill, which will provide for reform of statutory employment rights and industrial relations adjudication bodies, i.e. the Rights Commissioner Service, the Equality Tribunal, the Employment Appeals Tribunal, the National Employment Rights Authority's Inspection Service and the Labour Court. This reform has already commenced with the development of one combined complaint form for the majority of complaints (under all the relevant legislation) and the centralising of receipt of all complaints forms. Future reforms also include the establishment of an early resolution service (discussed further in Chapter 2).

What is my probationary period? My friends tell me it is six months. I have also been told I will be made permanent after such time. Is this true?
Probationary periods must be pre-defined in your terms of employment. Generally a six-month period is applicable, although an employer may extend that period to a maximum of twelve months. If the period is extended by your employer, you must be provided with notification in writing.

There is no automatic entitlement to be made permanent after a probationary period (six or twelve months), although it is important to note that there is legislation in place to provide the same or similar rights for part-time (Protection of Employees (Part-Time Work) Act 2001 – see Chapter 2), fixed-term (Protection of Employees (Fixed-Term Work) Act 2003 – see Chapter 2) and agency (Protection of Employees (Temporary Agency Work) Act 2012 – discussed above) workers compared to "permanent" employees in relation to entitlements to pro rata holiday entitlements, public holidays, access to pension schemes (subject to the eligibility criteria) and access to training and opportunities. Therefore, in essence, the only difference will be that of status of "permanent" employee as many comparable rights will be gained over time. You may not even be made permanent for at maximum four years, although in some cases this still may not be applicable. It would therefore be advisable to liaise with your employer to clarify the policy, or the policy may be pre-defined in your terms of employment.

What if I leave after six weeks? Must the employer still provide a contract of employment?

Yes. The minimum term of work completed for the provision of a contract of employment is one month. Even if the employee has completed one month in employment and has since left, the employer must provide a contract under the Terms of Employment (Information) Acts 1994–2001.

What if my employer wishes to change my terms and conditions of employment?

The employer must provide the employee with a written statement of changes to their terms of employment no later than one month after such changes have come into effect (section 5, Terms of Employment (Information) Act 1994). No written notification is required if these changes are through legislation or collective registered agreements.

It is important to note that if the changes are fundamental in nature it could be argued that there is a breach in contract (under contract law) and that these major changes in the terms and conditions of employment are so fundamental as to change the role and imply immediate redundancy (as the position is no longer) or invoke constructive dismissal (subject to compliance of exhausting all avenues of redress).

Alternatively, if the employee agrees with the changes, i.e. the changes are due to new technologies or varying business hours due to changes in the economic circumstances of the organisation, a new amended contract should be agreed and provided to the employee stating the changes. It is therefore essential for employers to ensure contract clauses provide for a wide scope of potential variances from the outset to prevent being locked in to certain terms. In contrast, an employee needs to be fully aware of the implications of all the terms and conditions of employment and how there may be scope for future change if it arises.

Do I have to sign a copy of my contract for it to be binding?
Normally the employee may be asked to sign a copy of the contract of employment but, in legal terms, this is not necessary to make it binding. When work commences, many terms and conditions of employment are accepted by implication through the employee's carrying out of the work. It would be advisable to receive a copy of your terms and conditions of employment in advance of commencement of work to ensure all issues are discussed and clarified.

I left my old job six months ago. How long must my old employer keep a copy of my terms and conditions of employment?
Your previous employer is under an obligation to keep a copy of your terms and conditions of employment for at least one year after your employment has ceased. This is required in case any disputes arise in the twelve months after termination of employment.

Under the Data Protection Acts 1998 and 2003, section 2(1)(c)(iv) states that "the data shall not be kept for longer than is necessary for that purpose or those purposes." Therefore, in relation to payroll, Revenue and personnel details, the maximum period of retention (from the date of the employee leaving) would be six years, in compliance with the Statute of Limitations Act 1957 and in compliance with the potential of a possible future financial audit.

How long after my employment has ceased can I make a complaint relating to that employment. To whom do I complain?

A complaint may be made up to six months (twelve months in some cases) after termination of employment or at any time during employment. A complaint may be made to the Workplace Relations Services for investigation or resolution.

At what age do I have to retire from work?

Your age of retirement is generally pre-defined in your contract of employment. In the majority of cases the age of retirement is 65, although some contracts may allow retirement at a lower age subject to certain conditions or options, i.e. years of service or optional early retirement, such as for the Gardaí. Therefore, if the retirement age is not stipulated in your contract of employment it could be argued that it is open ended, subject to you being capable, competent and 'fit' to do your job. In addition, if your employer tries to terminate your contract of employment on the grounds of age it could be argued you are being discriminated against on grounds of age under the Employment Equality Acts 1998–2011.

The retirement age will be a challenge for many employees in the coming years with the removal of the State (Transition) Pension for new applicants from 1 January 2014 (previously available to people aged 65). This will mean that the State Pension will only be available for those aged 66 from 1 January 2014. In addition, the payment age for the State Pension will increase to 67 in 2021 and 68 in 2028. This will potentially create a large void between the retirement age (as stipulated in your contract of employment) and the payment of the State Pension, which to date has not been clarified.

Does my employer have to recognise and negotiate with my union?

No, there is no obligation on an employer to have to recognise or negotiate with your union. Many employers may do so as part of collective agreements or through partnership. In addition, if there are two unions in a workplace an employer may only recognise one union and that may be the only union the employer may negotiate with. As an employee you have a right to join a union or terminate membership of a union. You cannot be discriminated against, treated differently or dismissed on the grounds of being a member of a union.

SUMMARY CHECKLIST: Terms of Employment

Ensure you have a contract of employment either before ☐
commencement of employment or within two months of
starting, clearly stating all express terms in compliance
with the Terms of Employment (Information) Acts 1994 and
2001.

Investigate any terms implied by custom and practice, or by ☐
collective registered agreement.

Seek clarification from your employer for any issues prior to ☐
or during employment and try to resolve them locally before
commencing external investigation (Workplace Relations
Services).

Ensure any amendments in your terms of employment are ☐
provided to you in writing within one month of the changes
being implemented.

Notice Periods

What is the minimum notice I must give my employer before leaving?

The minimum notice (under the Minimum Notice and Terms of Employment Acts 1973–2001) that an employee must give an employer is one week. This requirement may be increased according to the terms and conditions of your employment, e.g. one to three months. The notice period an employer must give an employee increases with the number of years of service, starting with the minimum of one week's notice if employed between thirteen weeks and two years up to a maximum of eight weeks (for more than fifteen years' service) (discussed later). Therefore it is essential to be aware of the notice period as defined in your terms and conditions of employment. If it is not clearly stated, then only one week's notice is required. If the employee refuses to comply with the notice period required to be given to their employer, an employer may pursue a civil action against the employee for breach of contract or an employer may deduct the notice period due from any outstanding pay due to the employee if there is an agreed clause in the contract or if the employee agrees to the deduction (section 5 of the Payment of Wages Act 1991), or, depending on the seniority of the position, the employer

may apply for an injunction to the courts preventing the employee commencing employment with a new employer.

I handed in my notice today and my employer asked me to leave straightaway. Can he do this?
Yes. The employer can ask you to leave straightaway without working out your notice. In return, he or she must then pay you in lieu of notice (this notice would be as defined in your contract, or it would be one week, if not). Your employer is not obliged under law to give you any written reference after you have left employment, i.e. character reference or otherwise. Some employers will facilitate a simple factual written reference confirming commencement date of employment, job title and date of cessation. Some employers may only provide an oral reference by phone. Many employers are apprehensive of providing written references or oral/telephone references as there are concerns in relation to data protection legislation, i.e. recorded/stored data. Employees have a right to and may request copies of the data stored or saved by future employers and any data must be accurate, up to date and in compliance with the legal responsibilities of the data controller (person who stores the data) and may lead to a claim for damages for the individual if the employer (past or future) fails to observe their duty of care in handling personal data.

Pay Cuts, Minimum Notice and Redundancy

My employer says that he wants all staff to take a 10 per cent pay cut. Can he do this?
When you commence employment, both you and your employer agree the terms and conditions of your employment, including those relating to your pay. Therefore the

terms and conditions can only change by agreement, that is, both parties must accept and agree to any changes. As an employee, you do not have to accept a reduction in pay, nor can your employer enforce a pay cut without your consent (unless you had a clause in your contract allowing for such reduction). If an employer reduces your pay without your consent, you can take an action regarding unlawful deduction (under the Payment of Wages Act 1991, section 5). If you are the only one who does not accept the pay cut and you dismissed for not accepting it, you can take an action under the Unfair Dismissals Acts 1977–1993, or, if your employer reduces your wage and you feel you have no alternative but to leave due to this deduction, you could take a constructive dismissal case.

In many cases the purpose of the proposed agreed reduction in salaries is to protect positions from redundancy, or the organisation from possibly closing down. Therefore a 10 per cent deduction may be agreed by all staff in the interests of the business and the employees. By not accepting a pay cut, this does not in any way specifically increase your risk of selection for redundancy, subject to the normal criteria. In addition, it is advisable to agree a review date, i.e. three or six months in the future, when it may be possible to review or amend the pay cut, or return to your original salary rate.

I took a case against my employer for deduction of my pay without my consent (through the Workplace Relations Services) and my case was heard by a Rights Commissioner. Even though I won my case I was not awarded the money back. Can this happen?
Yes, in theory an employer can be found in breach of section 5 of the Payment of Wages Act 1991, but if substantiated

evidence can be provided by the employer to justify, on financial and economic grounds, that the employer is unable to pay the "normal" rate, the Commissioner can find in his/her favour, and therefore not force the employer to pay the unpaid money back.

I work for a local authority and I am a member of a union. In the Croke Park Agreement the union agreed with the employer to change our payment method from weekly cheque to electronic payment. What if I don't want to change?

Employees who are union members are bound by agreements made on their behalf by the union even if they do not agree/accept or wish to comply with the agreement. For union members it is implicit in their acceptance of union agreements, as they were fundamentally written into their terms of employment, i.e. terms implied by collective agreements.

I work for a local authority and have not been a member of a union for over five years. In the Croke Park Agreement the union agreed with the employer to change our payment method from weekly cheque to electronic payment. What if I don't want to change?

As you are not represented by a union, you are not fundamentally required to comply with the unions' agreements made in your absence of representation. Therefore your employer is obliged to communicate with you any specific or proposed changes to your terms and conditions of employment. It is fundamental that your employer comply with all existing employment legislation and normal and existing procedures in place to communicate changes. In this case, the Payment of Wages Act 1991, section 2 clearly sets out the various different acceptable methods of payment, and therefore your employer can pay your wages in any of the methods clearly specified even if you disagree (discussed below).

Is my employer obliged to recognise a union? Can I make them?

No, an employer is not obliged to recognise a union or obliged to have to recognise or negotiate with a union on behalf of its members. It is important for employers to be clear in the terms and conditions of employment who can (or cannot) represent an employee, if required, in relation to any future disciplinary matters.

I am a civil servant; my pay was cut without my consent or agreement. Can this be done?

Yes, under section 5(1)(*a*) of the Payment of Wages Act 1991 your employer (the Government) can make a deduction from your pay which is "authorised to be made by virtue of any statute or any instrument made under statute", i.e. passed by legislation.

Lay-Offs and Short-Time

What is the difference between being laid off and short-time work? For what period do I have to be on short-time for me to claim redundancy?

Being laid off means being informed by your employer of a temporary cessation of work due to factors affecting the business. Short-time is when the employee's normal working week or earnings are reduced to less than half of what is normal. It is important in both cases for the employer to inform employees before the commencement of either lay-off or short-time and for employees to be aware of such situations. This is due to the fact that claims may be open to employees for redundancy if notice is not served.

It is possible to claim redundancy if the employee is either laid off or on short-time work for four consecutive weeks, or a broken series of six weeks within a thirteen-week period. If this is so, the employer must provide written notice to the employee of lay-off or short-time, or a written termination of their contract of employment. A RP9 form (available from www.redundancy.ie) can be used for three different situations:

- When an employer is giving notice to his/her employees of short-time or lay-off
- When employees seek redundancy after the requisite periods (i.e. four weeks of continuous lay-off or six weeks in any thirteen-week period)
- When an employer gives a counter-notice of redundancy to employees, stating that s/he will have work available

We have just returned to work after being on short-time and lay-off for over thirteen weeks. Do I still have an option to take redundancy?
You can seek redundancy if either:

- You have been have been laid off for a continuous period of four weeks, or a broken period of six weeks in a thirteen-week period, or
- You are on short-time (working for less than 50 per cent of your pay, or working less than 50 per cent of your working week) for a continuous period of four weeks, or a broken period of six weeks in a thirteen-week period

It is important to note that you can submit a claim for redundancy after these periods, or up to a maximum of four weeks after the short-time or lay-off stops, but if you do claim you will lose your right to get payment for notice (dependent on your years of service), as you will be classed as having left 'voluntarily'. If you submit your claim after this period, you are de-barred (not allowed to claim). If your employer did not provide you with notification of short-time or lay-off by providing you with the proper form (RP9), you can submit your claim for redundancy immediately.

Can my employer do anything to prevent me from claiming redundancy after I have given my notice?
Yes, your employer can counter-claim a redundancy notice within seven days of your notice by offering at least thirteen weeks of unbroken employment, commencing within four weeks of your notice. However, if a situation arises where, within the thirteen-week period, four or more consecutive weeks of short-time or lay-off occurs, the employee becomes re-eligible to claim redundancy.

Redundancy

What is the difference between redundancy and dismissal?
Dismissal is when the person is dismissed from work, generally in relation to disciplinary issues, or non-performance of duties. Redundancy is non-personal. It generally occurs when an employer requires fewer employees of a specific nature or with particular skills. Therefore a position can become redundant. Some of the grounds for redundancy may be as follows:

- The company goes into liquidation or receivership.
- The company is involved in re-organisation or restructuring.
- There is partial or total company shut-down.
- There is an economic recession.
- There is a reduction in the required number of qualified workers in a defined sector, or there is the continued need for employees with certain qualifications.

What is the difference between voluntary and compulsory redundancy?

Voluntary redundancy occurs when employees are asked to volunteer for redundancy (assuming they meet the criteria for eligibility above and the position is truly redundant). Compulsory redundancy is when employees are forced to take redundancy.

I have only been employed by my company for fifteen months; am I eligible for statutory redundancy payments?

No. The eligibility requirements for redundancy payments are as follows:

- You have two years of continuous service (104 weeks)
- You are employed in insurable employment
- You are aged over sixteen (no upper age cap)

If you are made redundant and you have less than two years' continuous service, you are not entitled to a redundancy payment, but you are entitled to notice (one week) or payment in lieu of notice, in addition to any outstanding pay and/or annual leave entitlements (pro rata).

What if I am due a bonus. Am I entitled to receive the payment?
It is essential to be aware of the terms and conditions, as defined in your contract, regarding payment in relation to your bonus. If you are in compliance with the terms and conditions of your contract of employment in relation to your bonus and your employer refuses to pay, then your employer is in breach of section 5 of the Payment of Wages Act 1991 and you can seek recovery of the payment through the single complaint form available on www.workplacerelations.ie for non-payment. "Wages" are defined as any fee, bonus, commission or expenses incurred in carrying out the work, or pension, payment or benefits-in-kind. Alternatively, an employee may take a civil case against the employer for breach of contract.

Is the minimum statutory redundancy taxable?
No, the minimum statutory redundancy is non-taxable, subject to a maximum weekly rate of €600 (gross pay and benefits-in-kind inclusive).

Can I be made redundant while I am out on sick leave?
Yes you can be made redundant while you are on sick leave. You are not protected from being served/notified of redundancy while you are on sick leave.

I have been with my company for five years. How much notice must they give me before dismissing me?
An employee must be in continuous service for at least thirteen weeks to be eligible for the minimum notice period of one week. Thereafter, the notice period increases with your years of service as follows:

Length of Service	Minimum Notice
13 weeks–2 years	1 week
2 years–5 years	2 weeks
5 years–10 years	4 weeks
10 years–15 years	6 weeks
More than 15 years	8 weeks

Payment can be made in lieu of notice. An online redundancy calculator is available from www.welfare.ie to provide assistance in calculating your redundancy payment due.

During the five years, the company laid me off for two months at the end of my first fixed-term contract. Is my service broken?
No. If you were laid off or your contract expired and then you were taken back on within 26 weeks, and you did not work with another employer, then your service is not broken. If, during your employment, a redundancy payment was paid to you, service is then broken. Strike action may also break continuous service.

Two years ago the company I work for was taken over by a multinational. Does my six years of service with my previous company still count towards my notice?
Your service is counted as continuous after a takeover by a new employer, and therefore all your previous service is added together for the purpose of minimum notice, that is, eight years entitles you to a minimum of four weeks' notice.

I have worked with my company for over six years, and I have been told today (Tuesday) that I am being let go on Friday. Can my employer do this?

Yes, your employer can do this as long as he pays you in lieu of the notice period you are entitled to. As you have been working for the company for over six years, you are entitled to either four weeks' notice or payment in lieu of notice. The date of cessation (on the P45) will be the date at the end of the notice period you are entitled to, i.e. four weeks from the date of notice.

I worked abroad for my employer for a period of time but then later returned to work in Ireland. Am I eligible for redundancy?

Under the Redundancy Payments Act 2003 employees who start work in a company abroad, work there for some time and are then transferred to the company or an associated company in the Republic of Ireland and work here for at least two years before being made redundant will have all of their service counted in calculating their statutory redundancy entitlements. Another factor to consider is in what jurisdiction you are employed regarding employment rights and dispute resolution.

If you commenced employment in Ireland and were then transferred to another jurisdiction, as long as your employment complies with the Social Welfare (Consolidated) Act 1993, and you are employed under insurable employment in Ireland (and your employer is making your contributions in Ireland), you are covered in full for all your service in relation to eligibility for redundancy. Section 4 of the Terms of Employment (Information) Act 1994 states that if an employee is required to work outside the State for 'more than one month they must be furnished with information in relation to the period of time to be employed outside the State, the currency in which they are to be paid, any benefits to be granted to them for working outside the State, and terms in relation to their return to Ireland. If there were any fundamental changes to your work conditions whilst you were away and you were not notified of these changes, you could argue that the changes may relate to a fundamental change in the terms and conditions of your employment and you may be able to seek immediate redundancy (as the original position is no longer) or invoke constructive dismissal (subject to compliance of exhausting all avenues of redress).

My employer has asked me to use up my annual leave as part of my notice period. Do I have to do this?
No, you are not required to use up your annual leave as part of your notice period unless you wish to do so. When you are given notice by your employer that your services are no longer required you are either required to work out your notice or you should receive payment in lieu of notice if your employer wishes you to cease employment immediately.

When you cease employment, you are entitled to be paid any outstanding accrued annual leave (pro rata) up to the date of termination of employment, as well as any outstanding pay due to you and any other payments, e.g. if your employer is paying you in lieu of notice. Therefore, if your employer has not paid you your outstanding pay, or has used your annual leave as part of your notice, you can take an action under the Payment of Wages Act 1991, section 5 (non-payment or unlawful deduction). Alternatively, if you have not been paid for your annual leave, you can take an action under the Organisation of Working Time Act 1997.

Our employer has given us two weeks' notice of redundancy. Is this sufficient? If I leave before the agreed date, can I still claim my redundancy payment?
The minimum notice required for redundancy is two weeks, and the maximum is eight weeks (if you have greater than fifteen years of service). Also, in the terms and conditions of your employment, the notice period may supersede the above minimum statutory requirements. This may be of benefit as part of negotiations for voluntary redundancy or agreements for redundancy over and above the minimum statutory requirements.

With reference to leaving before the agreed date, your employer will have provided you with a notice of dismissal (RP50 form), stating the date of dismissal. If you wish to request to leave before this date, you must provide your employer with notice in writing of this request on a special form (RP6 form). Your employer may accept or reject your offer.

If your employer rejects the offer, they may give you counter-notice, requesting you withdraw your offer and continue employment until the specified end date (specified on the RP6 form). If the employee unreasonably refuses to comply with the counter-notice, the employer may be able to contest the payment of redundancy. If the employer accepts the offer of the new end date, they will consent in writing (RP6 form). The date of dismissal will then become the date of the new notice (requested by the employee), and redundancy payments will be calculated on this new termination date.

Should my employer give me time off work to look for a new job during my notice period?

During the period of notice, the employee should be given reasonable paid time off during the two-week period prior to the cessation of employment to look for other work or to seek training for future alternative employment (as defined in section 7 of the Redundancy Payments Act 1979). The employer can request proof that the employee was actively seeking employment (section 7(4)). If the employer believes there is no valid proof of "actively" seeking employment s/he can submit a complaint to the Workplace Relations Services to seek recovery of payment and, if not recovered, can seek payment recovery through the courts as a "contract debt".

There are rumours in work about possible redundancies. Is there any financial support from Government to companies to prevent redundancies?

Previously the Employment Subsidy Scheme was available and was designed to support the maintenance of vulnerable jobs and prevent people from being made redundant. This scheme provided financial support of up to €6,370 per job for employees who worked between 21 and 35 hours per week, and up to €9,100 per job for employees who worked 35 hours or more per week. The scheme was available to employers who employed more than ten people. The scheme hoped to retain 72,000 jobs. Unfortunately, the scheme closed on 1 April 2011. For further information, check www.employmentsubsidy.ie.

A large number of employees in my firm are being made redundant. Should we not be informed in advance?

Yes. Under the Protection of Employment Act 1977, an

employer who is proposing collective redundancies is under an obligation to consult with unions or employees' bodies and notify the Minister for Jobs, Enterprise and Innovation a minimum of 30 days before such redundancies occur. Redundancies must not take place until at least 30 days after the Minister has been informed. The Protection of Employment (Exceptional Collective Redundancies and Related Matters) Act 2007 addresses cases of collective redundancies where specific situations apply, requiring the establishment of a new body, the Redundancy Panel. The Redundancy Panel will consider if "exceptional collective redundancies" exist. "Exceptional" redundancies occur when people are replaced in the same location or within the country with others who perform the same functions, and who have inferior terms and conditions of employment. If this claim is found valid, employees who were made redundant may be able to take action for unfair dismissal.

How soon can I be re-employed with the same employer after redundancy?
Technically there is no minimum period, subject to the fact that the position you return to must be fundamentally different (in terms and conditions and duties) to the position you were made redundant from. Otherwise it could be argued a valid redundancy did not take place. Alternatively, you may carry out some work in a self-employed/contractual capacity under which you are not an employee (contract for service). If this is the case, you are responsible for all your own tax affairs. If it can be found by either Revenue or the Department for Jobs, Enterprise and Innovation that a valid redundancy did not take place, you may have to repay anything received

through tax exemptions and/or refunds on the basis of redundancy, if these applied to you.

What issues must be discussed with the employee representative bodies?

These issues must include:

- Possibility of avoiding redundancies
- Selection of members for redundancy
- Reason for redundancies
- Categories of employees to be made redundant
- Method of calculation of redundancy payments (other than under the Redundancy Payments Act 2003)

How many people being made redundant constitutes 'collective' redundancies?

The following calculation must be considered in defining 'collective':

- At least 5, when the company employs more than 20 but less than 50
- At least 10, when the company employs more than 50 but less than 100
- At least 10 per cent, when the company employs more than 100 but less than 300
- At least 30, when the company employs more than 300

Does the 30-day rule apply if the company goes bankrupt?

The 30-day notice period (under the Protection of Employment Acts 1997–2007) is an obligation on an employer to inform the Minister for Jobs, Enterprise and Innovation in writing of proposed collective redundancies at least 30 days before any redundancy take place, as well as to inform employee representatives, who may consider or propose alternatives to collective redundancies. The 30-day rule only applies if the Minister so requests for cases of bankruptcy, liquidation or court order.

My son was completing an apprenticeship, but is being made redundant. Is he eligible for any payment?
An apprentice who is made redundant during their term of apprenticeship will qualify for redundancy, assuming they meet the normal criteria. However, if your son has completed his apprenticeship and is made redundant within one month of completion, redundancy will not be payable. If your son has completed more than one month's work after the completion of his apprenticeship, the total period of apprenticeship will be included in the calculation of his redundancy (normal eligibility rules apply).

I am on maternity leave at present. Can I be made redundant?
No, an employee on maternity, parental or force majeure leave cannot be given notice of redundancy until their return to work. Time on the above leave is included as reckonable for the purpose of calculating redundancy payments.

I am with my company over ten years and am now being made redundant. I was out sick from work for a large part of 2008. Will this affect my payment?
No, under the amendments to the Redundancy Act, only breaks in 'reckonable' service in the last three years will be taken into account. Therefore all other periods prior to three years ago are considered continuous in the calculation of redundancy payments.

If I was laid off work, is this counted in my service as regards calculation of redundancy payment? Also, I was sick from work six months ago (for a period of three months). Is this counted in my service?

All periods of lay-off in the last three years are not counted as a reckonable service. Periods of short-time are included. Any periods when you were on strike are considered non-reckonable. The first 26 weeks of sick leave (certified absence from work) are counted in full, but any period greater than 26 weeks is not reckonable. If you had an injury from work and you were absent due to the occupational injury, a full 52 weeks are counted as reckonable service in full, but any periods greater than that are excluded. Of course, any periods of absence or lay-off prior to the last three years are fully reckonable.

During my years of service with the company I was on unpaid maternity leave and I took a career break. Will these periods of absence affect my redundancy payment?

As we have seen, only periods of absence in the last three years of employment affect reckonable service. Unpaid additional maternity leave and a career break (if approved by the company) are all counted as 'reckonable' service.

I work with an employment agency. Am I still protected for redundancy?

Yes. Under the Redundancy Payments Act 2003, employees employed through an agency are covered for redundancy on the presumption that they meet the eligibility criteria and the agency itself pays their wages directly. This was re-enforced with the passing of the Protection of Employees (Temporary Agency Work) Act 2012 on 16 May 2012, with full effect from 5 May 2011.

I am on a fixed-term contract. Am I eligible for redundancy in any way?

Yes, you may be. Section 9(1)(*b*) of the Redundancy Payments Act 1967 states that an employee shall be taken to be dismissed by his employer if "where under the contract under which he is employed by the employer he is employed for a fixed term, that term expires without being renewed under the same or a similar contract." The Redundancy Payment Act 2003 section 6(*b*) also includes people on fixed-purpose contracts by stating they are employed for a "specified purpose (being a purpose of such a kind that the duration of the contract was limited but was, at the time of its making, incapable of precise ascertainment)". The legislation states that both fixed-term and fixed-purpose employees can seek redundancy if "that term expires or that purpose ceases without being renewed under the same or similar contract". This is of course subject to the normal eligibility requirements for redundancy.

Are there situations when my employer can refuse payment of redundancy by offering me an alternative job?

There are a number of situations that may allow your employer to retract or refuse redundancy. These are as follows:

- If the employee is offered a new or renewed contract with immediate effect, if the terms of the contract do not differ from the previous one and the employee accepts it
- If the employee is offered a new or renewed contract, within four weeks of the previous contract ending, if the terms of this contract differ from the previous contract and the employee accepts

In other situations, the employee may lose their entitlement to a redundancy payment, as follows:

- If the employee is offered a new or renewed contract, with effect from the date of the dismissal, if such terms do not differ from the previous contract and the employee unreasonably refuses the offer
- If the employee is offered a new or renewed contract, not later than four weeks after the date of dismissal, and the terms differ wholly or in part from the previous contract, the offer is deemed to be of suitable employment, and the employee unreasonably refuses the offer

The acceptance by an employee of a reduction in working hours or weekly pay (not less than half), for a period not greater than 52 weeks, shall not be taken as acceptance of an offer of suitable employment, and therefore does not remove the entitlement to seek redundancy.

My company is making me redundant after eight years' service. I started work with the company on 3 February 2003 and am paid €650 per week. What is the minimum statutory redundancy payment due to me? I was given notice on Friday, 24 August 2012 and was told to finish work on Friday, 31 August 2012. Will this affect my payment?
Prior to the Redundancy Payment Acts 1967–2003, different rates applied depending on age, i.e. whether you were under 41 or over 41 years of age. Since 10 April 2005, the new calculation method is much easier. The amended Act entitles the employee to two weeks' pay for every year of service, plus one additional bonus week. A percentage of the year in which you are made redundant, if applicable, is also counted. You should be provided with a RP50 form (available from www.welfare.ie) from your employer.

Therefore your payment is as follows:

Date of commencement of employment	3 February 2003
Date of notice of termination	24 August 2012
Date of termination*	31 August 2012
Gross weekly pay**	€600
Number of years in employment	9
Number of days in employment	213
Weeks due	19.16
Bonus week	1
Total weeks due	20.16
Lump sum due to employee	€12,096

*As only one week's notice was given, an additional three weeks' pay in lieu of notice should be paid.
**Maximum weekly redundancy payment (€600 per week), regardless of what you earn above this threshold.

In Budget 2012, the Minister reduced the rebate the employer can seek from the Department of Social Protection from 60 per cent to 15 per cent (since January 2012). Therefore, the actual cost to the company is €10,281.60 (€12,096 – €1,814.40). From January 2013 (under Budget 2013), the remaining rebate to employers of 15 per cent will be removed completely, therefore the employer will not be due any refund whatsoever for redundancies of employees thereafter. In this case no tax is due on the payment received by the employee as it is the statutory minimum payment. A RP50 form must be completed and returned to the Redundancy Payment Section of the Department of Social Protection within six months of the redundancy. Claims are primarily submitted online and are processed quicker than the traditional 'hard-copy' applications. For further information check out the redundancy calculator on www.welfare.ie.

My employer wants us to reduce our working week to three days a week (from five days per week). What are the implications for our employment rights?

If you are asked to reduce your working week to a three-day week (from five days per week), this is purely a voluntary decision. This will affect any possible future redundancy payments, as the redundancy rate will be set as your new weekly rate. Also, in turn, this will affect any financial assistance from the Department of Social Protection, as you have voluntarily reduced your working week, and therefore are not 'unemployed' for those other days.

If your employer reduces your working week (from five to three days, in this case) on a temporary or permanent basis, this will not affect your possible rate of redundancy, and you can seek assistance from the Department of Social Protection for the additional two days per week (if on a temporary or permanent basis), subject to the Department's eligibility requirements. In Budget 2012 the Minister announced that from July 2012 the current six-day welfare week will be reduced to a five-day welfare week. In addition, from 2013 Sunday work will be taken into account for assessment for Jobseeker's payments (Benefit and Allowance).

My working week was reduced during the year by my employer. If I am offered redundancy, will my wage be calculated on my current or previous wages?

If, prior to redundancy, your hours and rate of pay were reduced, and you continuously sought a return to full-time work, your redundancy payment will be calculated at your prior full-time payment rate. If, however, an employee was on a reduced working week and pay for over 52 weeks, and s/he accepted these new terms as being the norm, without requesting a return to full-time work, the new lower rate will be the assessable rate for redundancy. If the employee specifically requested a reduced working week, and the change was not forced upon them, the new lower rate of pay is applicable for redundancy.

Should I get my redundancy payment when I leave or after I leave?

You should receive your payment in full from your employer at the time you finish employment with your employer. You should only sign the P50 form confirming receipt of payment when you actually receive your payment.

My employer says he only has to give me 40 per cent of what I am entitled to as I can get the 60 per cent rebate from the Government. Is this true?

No, this is not true. Since Budget 2012 (1 January 2012) the rate of rebate for employers for all redundancies reduced from 60 per cent to 15 per cent. Your employer is obliged to pay you your redundancy in full, and then he can seek the 15 per cent rebate from the Department of Social Protection himself.

What if my employer cannot afford to pay me my redundancy pay, what should I do?

If your employer cannot afford to pay you your redundancy at the time of leaving, there are alternative arrangements in place, subject to confirmation of the redundancy by your employer. The Department of Social Protection has an arrangement in place where the Department will make the payment from the Social Insurance Fund subject to the employer providing detailed information proving inability to pay. The evidence required would include recently audited accounts or a statement of affairs signed by an auditor/accountant as evidence. This would mean, if approved, the Department of Social Protection would become a preferential creditor to your employer, and therefore the Department of Social Protection would rank as one of the first to be paid when the business accounts are resolved/liquidated.

My rate of pay varies, depending on commission, etc. How is my rate calculated for the purpose of redundancy?
Firstly, you go back thirteen weeks from the date of termination of employment. You then go back a further 26 weeks (i.e. a total of 39 weeks). Then you calculate the total payment for the 26-week period (if there are 'blank' weeks or weeks you did not work, we exclude them, and go back the requisite number of weeks), and divide it by the total number of hours worked, i.e. to get the hourly rate. This hourly rate is multiplied by the number of hours normally worked in a week to get your redundancy rate. However, if you have no normal working hours, you take the average (including commission) over the last 52 weeks.

My father was due to receive his redundancy, but died suddenly last week. Does his family have any claim?
If an employee dies before the proposed dismissal date, not having received a redundancy payment, payment will still be due and will be based on his or her service up to the time of death. It is important to consider whether your father had either accepted or refused his employer's offer of renewal or re-engagement before the proposed dismissal date and if the offer had been withdrawn before his death. If the offer still stands, no redundancy entitlement will arise from the claim. Similarly, no redundancy claim

will be eligible if your father gave notice to his employer by way of short-time or lay-off (RP9 form) and died within seven days of giving the notice.

What if my employer did not provide me with a RP50 form, or even certify my redundancy?

Firstly, you will be required to seek clarification from your employer regarding your cessation of employment (RP77 form). This form is used either to seek clarification that you have been made redundant, if you have not been paid the correct full lump sum entitlement from the employer, or, if your case has been awarded by the Employment Appeals Tribunal (EAT), to seek payment from your employer. If the employer accepts there is a valid redundancy s/he should then complete a RP50 form (redundancy certificate). If the employer ignores the application over a reasonable period of time (on average fourteen days) you should then submit a claim to the Workplace Relations Services, using the form available on www.workplacerelations.ie, to seek a hearing for redundancy (and/or notice).

If my employer does not pay my redundancy payment can I still receive a payment?

If the employer has accepted your request to confirm redundancy (RP77 and RP50 forms), and can't pay because of inability to pay, and provides substantial information to the Department of Social Protection, you can forward your RP50 form to the Department for payment from the Social Insurance Fund.

If, however, your employer did not accept the redundancy (RP77 form), and you submitted your claims to the Workplace Relations Services for redundancy, and you received a favourable hearing, you can then submit your claim against your employer for payment (RP77 form). If your employer can't pay, and s/he provides substantial information supporting that fact and it is approved by the Department of Social Protection, you can submit the RP50 form, with a copy of the favourable decision from the EAT, to the Department to seek payment from the Social Insurance Fund.

My employer has gone bust and can't afford to pay me my notice period. What can I do?
Under the Protection of Employees (Employers' Insolvency) Acts 1984–2004, as amended by the European Communities (Protection of Employees (Employers' Insolvency)) Regulation (SI 630/2005), we need to determine what the official status of the employer is. Therefore, under this Act, employees can only be assisted if the employer's business is:

- In liquidation
- In receivership
- Legally bankrupt
- Insolvent under the legislation of another EU member state; or the employer is deceased and the estate is being administered under the relevant legislation

The Insolvency Payments Scheme does not cover situations where the business simply shuts down and does not become legally insolvent. Generally, claims are submitted to the liquidator or receiver in charge of the business. When the liquidator or receiver receives the claim (via the old EIP1 form) they will verify its validity and, if approved, it will be forwarded to the Department of Social Protection for payment from the Social Insurance Fund. Alternatively, claims can be submitted online at www.welfare.ie (Online Insolvency Claim Form). Upon approval, payment is made to the liquidator or receiver, and is then paid to the employee, normal tax and PRSI reductions applying. A maximum of eight weeks' arrears only is applicable through the Insolvency Fund. The Insolvency Payments Scheme also protects employees' outstanding contributions to occupational pension schemes which an employer may have deducted from wages but not paid into the schemes. Unpaid contributions to an occupational pension scheme on the employer's books may also be paid from the fund, subject to certain limits. The scheme applies to outstanding pension contributions for up to a year prior to the date of insolvency. If there is no liquidator or receiver appointed, you may wish to make your complaint via the online single complaints form through www.workplace relations.ie.

What if my appeal is rejected by the liquidator or receiver? What do I do?
You will then need to submit a claim to the Workplace Relations Services by completing a form (available from www.workplacerelations.ie or a T1C form, available from www.eatribunal.ie if you are appealing the decision of the Minister for Social Protection under the Protection of Employees (Employer's Insolvency) Acts 1984 to 2001). It is important you fill out the form correctly and submit the official business name (not the name of the owner). The official business name can be obtained from your previous payslips, P60, P45 or from the Companies Registration Office (www.cro.ie). A hearing date will be set (upon receipt of your claim), and, upon determination of the facts, a decision will be made.

Subject to the Workplace Relations Services accepting the validity of your case, you can submit your claim as above (EIP1 form online), or alternatively you may need to seek an enforcement order for payment through the District Court.

The company I worked for just went bust and we have not been paid for three weeks. Can we get any of our back pay?
If the company has gone bankrupt, you may claim under the Insolvency Payments Scheme (as above) in relation to payments due. The scheme covers arrears of wages, sick pay (if applicable), holiday pay and pay in lieu of notice. Also included may be any outstanding payment due under any industrial relations disputes. Claims are generally submitted first to the liquidator or receiver for payment. The maximum wage limit per week is €600. Such payment is made (upon approval) from the Social Insurance Fund, and in some cases may receive outstanding contributions to pension and occupational pension schemes, subject to limitations.

I turned up for work today and there was simply a note on the door saying the company had closed. Where do I go and what do I do?
The first thing to do is either contact your company's head office for further details or contact your trade union or the Companies Registration Office (www.cro.ie) to see if the company has appointed a liquidator or receiver. If they have, they should be able to provide you with their details and you can contact them directly to organise outstanding payment. If one has not been appointed you can submit a complaint form to www.workplacerelations.ie to seek payment of monies due.

The company I worked for closed down and re-opened under a different name but is still the same company in essence. Do I have any recovery?
Yes, you may. If it can be proved that it is owned by the same or similar directors and/or owners and is carrying out the same trade/activities, it could be argued it is a transfer of business (under the Protection of Employees on Transfer of Undertakings Regulations 2003) and it could be argued you should retain and transfer your service to the new employer or it could be argued as unfair dismissal (under the Unfair Dismissals Act 1997–1993) as you were intentionally dismissed for the purpose of avoidance of employment (both discussed later).

SUMMARY CHECKLIST: Redundancy

Is it a valid redundancy or an unfair dismissal? ☐

Are you covered under the Act, regarding your employment? ☐

Was redundancy voluntary or compulsory? ☐

Were you laid off or on short-time? For how long? ☐

Can your employer counter-claim? Is there further work available? ☐

Was there a valid alternative position offered and accepted? ☐

Has the employer complied with the relevant forms? ☐

How long have you worked for the company? ☐

Have you checked the terms and conditions of your employment regarding minimum terms of notice for either you or your employer? ☐

Were you given proper notice? ☐

Were you given reasonable time off to look for a new job? ☐

Does your employer have the money to pay your redundancy payment? ☐

Has your employer paid you in full for monies due? ☐

Will you have to work out your notice or will you be paid in lieu ☐ of notice?

If your company was taken over, did you count all your years' ☐ service?

If your service was broken with your employer, how long was ☐ the gap, and did you work for someone else during that time?

Has your company gone into liquidation or has your employer ☐ ceased trading, or is he or she simply not willing to pay you?

Interviews and Offers of Employment

I completed a job interview two weeks ago. Although I was certain that I did well, I didn't get the job. Am I entitled to my scorecard and feedback from the company? The company is just ignoring my calls. What can I do?

You have no automatic entitlement to records of your scorecard or feedback from prospective employers. Some companies, as part of their policy, may provide certain feedback upon request. Alternatively, you may be able to seek a copy of any scorecards or written comments recorded by the interviewer(s) from that interview under section 4 of the Data Protection Acts 1988 and 2003. You may also make a request for information classed as an 'examination' (section 4(6)). An examination means any test of knowledge, skill or ability, and is not restricted to State examinations. It is important to submit your application for such information upon receipt of your result. You must clearly state your request in writing, referring to the relevant legislation (and section). Your request must be specific in detail and refer to the date, time and location of your examination, and other specific data required – date and location of interview, post applied for, etc. It may be advisable to include a fee of €6.35 (the maximum fee payable under the Act). The company must provide the information within 40 days (or 60 days for a request under section 4(6), at the latest). It is important to note that only records or notes relating to you will be provided (and not those of other candidates), although section 4(4) allows the provision of as much information as possible without identifying other individuals. Data concerning other individuals may only be released with their consent.

In a number of cases, employers may destroy information relating to such interviews shortly after the selection and appointment of the successful candidates. It would therefore be advisable to submit your request promptly. For further information check the website of the Data Protection Commissioner at www.dataprotection.ie.

I was sent a job offer by post last week. Yesterday I received a phone call from the company to say that the position has been withdrawn. What can I do?
Your employment rights only commence from the first day of your employment. Therefore, in your situation, as you have not commenced employment with your new employer there is no employment legislation to protect you. Questions to consider in relation to such a case include:

- Was the job position subject to references?
- Did your reference check come back negative?
- Did you contact your referees to check the details given?
- Were you formally offered the position?
- Did you receive the offer in writing?
- Did you verbally accept the offer?
- Did you accept the written offer within the required time frame?

- Are there grounds for a case for discrimination (under the nine grounds laid out in the Employment Equality Act 1998)?
- Was the position in a sector that is subject to economic downturn?

It is also important to consider if you handed in your resignation to your current employer, and if resignation was accepted. That resignation cannot be reversed (unless at the discretion of your employer).

Therefore it may be advisable to seek legal opinion in relation to a potential breach of contract by your proposed new employer, and not under any employment legislation.

Change of Ownership (Transfer of Business)

I have worked with the same company for five years. We are being taken over by a large multinational. Do my terms and conditions remain the same?

Under the Protection of Employees on Transfer of Undertakings Regulations 2003, employees' terms and conditions of employment are protected and continue upon the transfer of ownership until the date of termination or any future collective agreements are entered into. This may not be applicable in relation to all pension schemes, although certain schemes are protected under the Pensions Acts 1990–2003. The Transfer of Undertakings (Pensions) Bill proposes to increase the statutory basis of pension provisions (including the Transfer of Undertakings Directive). There has been no progress with this Bill since the dissolution of the last Government on 1 February 2011.

The term 'transfer' is generally defined as the change of ownership of a business when the business continues the same or similar activities.

Can I be dismissed because of a change of ownership?

Generally, employees are protected from dismissal under transfer of ownership, although dismissals may be allowable for economic or organisational reasons, requiring changes in the workforce. In summary, what this means is that, if the proposed new owner wishes to make changes to the way the business is run and how departments are set up, and if the continuity of certain sections of the business does not make business sense, they can decide to make radical changes. However, if an employee is not selected for continuity of employment under the transfer of ownership, they may consider taking an unfair dismissal case against their old employer, and taking a case against the new employer under the Transfer of Undertakings Regulations 2003.

How soon should we be informed about the proposed change of ownership?

Employees (and/or their representatives) should be informed at least 30 days before the proposed transfer from the existing employer to the new employer (owner). Discussion is essential to ensure full transparency for all employees and a smooth transition of operations, including continuity of terms and conditions of employees.

SUMMARY CHECKLIST: Change of Ownership

When the company 'changed hands', did your employment conditions continue as normal?	☐
Were you dismissed as part of a takeover?	☐
Were you informed in advance of a takeover?	☐

Unfair Dismissal

How long must you be in continuous service before you can take an unfair dismissal case?
The general rule is that you must be in continuous employment for at least twelve months before you can take an action for unfair dismissal. However, the minimum qualifying criteria can be removed for any of the following reasons:

- Dismissal in relation to a fixed-term contract (under the Protection of Employees (Fixed-Term Work) Act 2003)
- Dismissal in relation to an employee's pregnancy or exercising a right to maternity leave
- Dismissal because the employee exercises or proposes to exercise a right to adoptive leave, parental leave, the national minimum wage or carer's leave
- An employee's trade union membership

If I am employed for less than one year, but do not fall within the above categories, is there anything I can do?
Yes, possibly. You may be able to take an action under the Industrial Relations Act 1969. Recommendations from these outcomes are non-binding (non-enforceable), although both parties normally comply under the principle of good faith.

My employer did not give me a written reason for my dismissal. Is she legally required to?
Your employer, upon your request, must provide you with a reason in writing within fourteen days. The employer may not be bound by this specific reason in a case for unfair dismissal.

My employer takes me on for six-month periods with a break of two months between them. He says they are separate periods. Is this true?

No. If your employer intentionally breaks your service for the purpose of avoiding employment rights, this service may be considered as collective continuous service (Unfair Dismissals (Amendment) Act 1993, section 3(*b*)). Other factors to consider are whether or not another employer employed you during these periods and if the break in service was no greater than 26 weeks (6 months) or the reason for the 'break period' was wholly or partly for the purpose of avoidance of liability (section 3(*b*)(iv)).

I was dismissed last week for serious misconduct. Should I not have been paid in lieu of my minimum notice?

No, your employer has the right to terminate employment without notice payment if you are dismissed on the grounds of serious misconduct, as defined in your disciplinary procedure. You may wish to internally appeal this decision and, subject to such appeal, the dismissal decision and notice may be reversed.

I work for my father on the family farm and live in the family home on the land. We had a difference of opinion last week and he dismissed me. He says he does not have to give me my minimum terms of notice under the Act. Is he right?

Yes, your father is fully compliant with the Minimum Notice and Terms of Employment Acts 1973–2001. There are a number of categories of workers who do not fall within the regulations of the Act. These are as follows:

- Established civil servants
- Members of the Permanent Defence Forces (except temporary staff in the Army or nursing service)

- Members of the Garda Síochána
- Seamen signing in under the Merchant Shipping Act
- Immediate family of the employer, provided they live with him or her and are employed in the same private house or farm

I work for the Garda Síochána. Can I take a case for unfair dismissal?
In general, no, but members of the Defence Forces and Gardaí can take cases on grounds of dismissal in relation to parental, force majeure, adoptive and carer's leave. Other specific grounds for a valid case may be related to pregnancy or maternity leave. Therefore it is important to check if you are eligible to take a case prior to your application, and what, if any, limited grounds you can submit your case under.

I am currently on probation with my employer but she has dismissed me. Can she do this?
Yes, an employer can dismiss an employee during their probationary period, assuming the contract is in writing and the period of probation or training is one year or less and is clearly stated. Obviously, if dismissal is on grounds of pregnancy and/or exercising your right to leave during probation, the employer cannot dismiss you during the probation period.

I was on strike last week with my colleagues. They have since returned to work but I have been sacked. Do I have a case for unfair dismissal?
Yes, you may have a case on the grounds that your colleagues returned to work and the presumption that you were dismissed because of your participation in the strike.

A case for unfair dismissal is applicable if the remainder of your colleagues returned to work after the strike or if your colleagues were dismissed but later reinstated.

I am an apprentice with FÁS and was told I am being dismissed. Can this be true?
A dismissal may be fair if it occurs during the six-month period immediately after commencing the apprenticeship or within one month of completion of the apprenticeship. Alternatively, you may have a valid case for unfair dismissal if you are dismissed on grounds of leave or pregnancy.

I am training as a nurse. Do I have similar rights during apprenticeship as FÁS apprentices?
The Unfair Dismissals Acts 1977–1993 do not apply to trainee nurses or other specified paramedical employments, except only on grounds of leave or pregnancy.

I am coming up to the end of a one-year contract and will be dismissed at the end of the contract. Can I take a case for unfair dismissal?
Unfortunately you may not be able to take a case if your employer has conformed to the following requirements:

- Provided a contract in writing
- The contract was signed by both parties.
- The contract contains a specific clause stating that the Unfair Dismissals Acts 1977–1993 are not applicable upon the termination of the contract.

However, you may have a case if these conditions are not present and the specific purpose of the contract was not stated at the outset (section 3(*b*)(iii) of the Unfair Dismissal (Amendment) Act 1993 – "the dismissal consisted only of the expiry of the term of the subsequent contract without the term being renewed under the contract").

I was dismissed today for taking and eating an item from the shop during working hours and not paying for it. Can my employer do this?

The important issue to note here is what the disciplinary procedure (if available) in your company is. The disciplinary procedure should clearly lay out serious and non-serious incidents, and disciplinary action to be taken.

Some employers state actions of gross misconduct that are clear and direct reasons for dismissal, i.e. theft, physical attack, etc. Other actions may be classed as non-serious incidents, i.e. misconduct (lateness, absenteeism, etc.) and may be punishable in a less formal capacity, e.g. by verbal or written warning. It is essential therefore for an employer to set down the clear parameters of each breach in the disciplinary procedure and the implications of breach of misconduct or gross misconduct.

It is essential, therefore, to be aware of the disciplinary procedure and the seriousness of possible actions. All evidence may be used in cases of unfair dismissal.

In summary, your employer may be able to dismiss you if valid grounds exist and they are fair and reasonable. If your employer does not have a grievance and disciplinary procedure the Code of Practice – Grievance and Disciplinary Procedures, SI 146/2000, is available, which should be used as a template. The procedure should always allow for an appeal of any decision, and any appeal should be heard by parties for the employer who have had no part in the original decision. This is to ensure a system of fairness for the hearing. If an appeal is refused, this could be a determining factor if the complaint proceeds to the Workplace Relations Services.

Is there not a 'three strikes and you're out' policy or must there be a verbal and two written warnings before dismissal?

This is a common misconception regarding a standard disciplinary procedure. Although many organisations have standard disciplinary procedures, such procedures may vary from company to company, and therefore it is essential for all employees to be fully aware of such procedures.

A copy of procedures should be readily available or included in your terms and conditions of employment. Therefore your employer does not have to issue a verbal warning and two written warnings in any or every case but s/he must follow their own internal disciplinary procedures or the recommended guidelines (stated above).

My employer dismissed me today. Is it up to me to prove my case for unfair dismissal?

No, generally the burden of proof is on the employer to prove that the dismissal was fair and reasonable. Alternatively, the burden of proof shifts if you leave your employment and claim constructive dismissal.

What is constructive dismissal?

Constructive dismissal is when you leave your employment on grounds that your conditions of employment have become so difficult it was impossible to remain employed with your employer. It is your duty in this case as an employee to exhaust every avenue possible with the employer to try to resolve any issues in the workplace before leaving their employment on constructive dismissal grounds. This means fully exploring proper procedures, and a willingness to accommodate a reasonable resolution and explore other areas such as mediation or conciliation. If all avenues have then been explored you may wish to submit a claim for constructive dismissal.

So what are valid grounds for dismissal?
The valid grounds for dismissal are as follows:

- The employee's conduct
- The employee's capability
- Competence of the employee at the work s/he is employed to do
- Qualification – if you lied in relation to your qualification level or you did not reach the required qualification level for the job required

I was dismissed from work because of a complaint received about me. Should I have the right of appeal?
Yes, you should be made aware of the complaint, and have a right to see the complaint and have an opportunity to present a case in your defence prior to any disciplinary action. Generally, an employee may be suspended with pay pending an investigation, although this may depend on your terms of employment. In general, any investigation should be resolved in full within a reasonable period of time. (Investigations that take too long may assist your case if further legal action is required.) Dependent on the outcome of the case, and the reason for your dismissal, you should have a right to appeal, and any appeal should be heard by a party independent of the original hearing. It is essential that the employer follows all the correct steps

clearly laid down in the disciplinary procedure. If you are still unhappy, you may have a right to take further legal action.

If I made a complaint or statement in relation to another employee can I request that it is in confidence?
It is important to note that when making a formal complaint you may be required to put it in writing and to ensure the complaint is not untrue or made out of spite as, if proven, action may be taken against you, the complainant. The person against whom you are making a complaint has a right, in the interests of fairness and transparency, to see a copy of the complaint in their defence, and be able to respond accordingly if asked to do so at a disciplinary hearing.

In addition, as a complainant, you have a right to voice a complaint or grievance without being discriminated against or victimised for doing so; if this occurs you can make a complaint under employment equality legislation to the Workplace Relations Services.

Alternatively, if a complaint is made and you require the complaint to be made in confidence, it may impair the employer from divulging some of the facts (to help protect your identity) and so may reduce the impact of the evidence against the person you are complaining about. This could limit the scope of possible disciplinary action unless there are clear facts available to present to the accused person, to which they have a right of reply, in the interests of fairness.

If the complaint is of a criminal nature, your employer will be required to provide substantive evidence or put in place preventative measures to investigate the complaint and ensure sufficient evidence is in place to take disciplinary action or refer for prosecution to the Gardaí.

Finally, the Protected Disclosure in the Public Interest Bill proposes to protect workers in all sectors (public and private) against punishment in circumstances where they make a disclosure of information relating to wrongdoing which comes to their attention in the workplace. The proposed legislation will highlight the responsibility of employers to put in place internal procedures to investigate whistleblowing and to develop an organisational culture that supports whistleblowing in order to identify potential wrongdoing and take appropriate corrective action at the earliest possible stage.

Section 20 of the Criminal Justice Act 2011 states "an employer shall not penalise or threaten penalisation against an employee, or cause or permit any other person to penalise or threaten penalisation against an employee for making a disclosure or for giving evidence in relation to such disclosure in any proceedings relating to a relevant offence" and reporting the matter to the Gardaí. The offences reported can be in relation to banking, investment and financial activities, breaches of company law, money laundering, terrorism, theft, fraud, taking part in a pyramid scheme or destroying data.

If I wish to take a case for unfair dismissal, what outcome can I request?
There are three options regarding the outcome you request:

- Reinstatement – this means returning to your old job with the same terms and conditions you had before you took the case. This would also include any increases or increments due to you under the contract during the intervening months.

- Re-engagement – this means returning to your old job or an alternative position (according to what the hearing body decides) from the time of outcome of the case.
- Compensation – this is dependent on whether you have commenced employment with another employer or not at the time the case is investigated. If you have commenced employment with another employer immediately after dismissal or shortly afterwards, you may only be awarded up to a maximum of four weeks' compensation. If you have not been employed up to and including the case hearing, the factors that must be considered are:
  - ° Contributory negligence – if the employee was proportionately responsible (percentage-wise) for the dismissal
  - ° Actions of the employer during any grievance or disciplinary procedures commenced with the employee during employment
  - ° Redundancy payments
  - ° Any other factors dependent on the case, e.g. has the employee been actively seeking employment?

Social welfare payments and tax rebates (if applicable) received by the former employee during the dismissal period are not assessed in the calculation of compensation.

What is the maximum award due under the Unfair Dismissals Acts 1977–1993?
The maximum award due under the Acts is 104 weeks' (2 years') salary. Full compensation is not generally awarded. Each case is taken on its own merits and takes into consideration all factors.

Is my employer obliged to give me a reference?

No, your employer is not obliged under legislation to provide you with a written character reference. They can simply provide any prospective employer with confirmation of your employment (start and end date, job title or position and/or duties). Under the Employment Law Compliance Bill 2008 your employer will be obliged to provide you with a statement clearly stating the duration and nature of your work, and a general description of the work involved. The employer will also be obliged to provide you with any personal documents and property belonging to you. There has been no progress with this Bill since the dissolution of the last Government on 1 February 2011.

If your reference is stored on file by your employer or prospective employer, you may have access to it, unless it was provided on a confidential basis and such policy was stated.

Does compensation cover legal fees?

Firstly, there is no requirement for you to have legal representation as you can represent yourself at employment redress hearings (if required), although if you prefer to have legal representation you can do so, but at your own expense. Legal aid is not available in employment redress cases. Therefore, compensation awards do not cover legal fees. No legal fees are awarded for or against in any cases. Costs may be set against an employee in extreme circumstances when cases are unwarranted or unjustified. Therefore if you lose your case you will be liable for your own legal costs/representation (and not the other side, as in normal court hearings).

SUMMARY CHECKLIST: Unfair Dismissal

How long have you worked for your employer?	☐
Are you eligible to take a case against your employer?	☐
What was the reason for dismissal?	☐
What was your employer's grievance and disciplinary procedure?	☐
Did your employer comply with the relevant steps in the procedure?	☐
Did you explore all the avenues before leaving employment (constructive dismissal)?	☐
If taking an action which option did you choose and why?	☐
What factors may impinge on assessing the case?	☐

Wages, Training and Workers' Permits

I believe the national minimum wage is €8.65 per hour. Why do I receive less?
Certain employees are allowed to be paid less than the national minimum wage. The national minimum wage (€8.65 since 1 July 2007 and restored since 1 July 2011) for an experienced adult worker is applicable to all employees, i.e. full-time, part-time, temporary and casual employees. Other rates are in the table below:

Category	Minimum Hourly Rate of Pay
Under 18	€6.06 per working hour
1st year from date of 1st employment over age 18 (employment experience prior to 18 not included)	€6.92 per working hour
2nd year from date of 1st employment over age 18 (employment experience prior to 18 not included)	€7.79 per working hour

(Continued)

(Continued)	
Category	Minimum Hourly Rate of Pay
1st one-third period of structured training or study over age 18 undertaken in normal working hours	€6.49 per working hour
2nd one-third period of structured training or study over age 18 undertaken in normal working hours	€6.92 per working hour
3rd one-third period of structured training or study over age 18 undertaken in normal working hours	€7.79 per working hour
Experienced adult worker	€8.65 per working hour

Employers can submit a claim for "inability to pay" under section 41 of the National Minimum Wage Act 2000. In this case, approval must be granted by the Labour Court pending an agreement with all employees and subject to other conditions. The exemption shall be for not less than three months and no greater than twelve months. Only one exemption is available per employer. In addition, this power may be extended to employees covered under Registered Employment Agreements (REAs) and Employment Regulation Orders (EROs), as amended by the Industrial Relations (Amendment) Act 2012 (discussed above).

What is structured training and how long does it last?
Structured training must involve:

- Study or skills training aimed at enhancing work performance
- At least 10 per cent of your normal working week allocated to directed study or training, away from day-to-day

operational work pressures. Such training may in some situations take place outside of your normal working week.

- Assessment and certification documentation or written confirmation of your completion of the course of study or training

Each one-third period (as seen in the table above) must be at minimum one month and no longer than twelve months.

How much of an increase am I entitled to every year? Is it the cost of living increase?
Contrary to common belief, there is no automatic entitlement to a pay increase every year.

My employer provides me with accommodation (board and lodgings). I receive €285 per week (gross) after taking into account accommodation costs. I work 39 hours per week. Am I being underpaid?
In calculating your hourly rate, we must consider the gross amount (before tax and PRSI). We must also take into consideration any other factors including shift premium, bonuses or commission (productively related) or piece or incentive rates. Overtime, Sunday, unsocial or public holiday premiums are not taken into account. Certain categories are excluded in relation to the national minimum wage (close relatives and apprentices). Higher rates may apply in relation to certain trades or sectors of employment. Board and lodgings are assessed at €54.13 per week (€7.73 per day). If you only receive board, the rate is €32.14 per week (€4.60 per day) and lodgings are assessed at €21.85 per week (€3.14 per day).

Presuming no other payments are being received, your situation is assessed as follows:

Experienced Adult Worker	
€8.65 per working hour (39 hours per week)	€337.35 per week
Board and lodgings (€54.13 per week)	−€54.13 per week
Gross pay	€283.22 per week

Therefore it would appear your employer is complying with the national minimum wage in paying you €285 per week. If you are unsure as to your hourly rate of pay, you are entitled to a written statement from your employer (upon your written request to him or her) only if your average hourly rate is below €12.45 per working hour. S/he must reply within four weeks or else face a possible criminal charge. You must not be victimised or discriminated against in seeking such a statement of your rights.

What is the situation in relation to Romanian and Bulgarian workers since the expansion of the EU? Can they work here with a work permit?
On 17 July 2012 (in advance of the maximum restricted period until 1 January 2014) the Government decided to end restrictions on Bulgarians and Romanians accessing the Irish labour market with effect from 1 January 2012. This means that nationals of Romania and Bulgaria no longer need an employment permit to work in Ireland.

Prior to the new ruling, since 1 January 2007, Romanian and Bulgarian workers still required a work permit to work in Ireland (although, if they had one for twelve months prior to 31 December 2006, one was not required).

Regarding work permits in general, the ruling has been in place since 1 June 2009 that there will be no new work permits for those earning less than €30,000 per year. In addition, work permits for work riders (horse riding), domestic workers and lorry drivers will no longer be issued, as well as those for general, administrative and production staff and hotel, tourism and catering staff (excluding chefs). The fee for renewal of work permits has also been increased. A working visa/work authorisation is usually valid for two years and then for a further three years (upon renewal). Since 28 August 2009, if you have worked for five consecutive years on a work permit you will no longer need a work permit to work in Ireland. When you have been legally living and working in Ireland for five years on a work permit you can apply for long-term residence to the Irish Naturalisation and Immigration Service (INIS) (www.inis.gov.ie). The work permit is granted to the employee, and the employer cannot retain documents or deduct recruitment costs from pay. This was re-enforced through the European Temporary Agency Directive (adopted in June 2008 and which came into full effect on 5 December 2011), which provides that it is an offence for an employment agency to charge a fee to facilitate an agency worker commence direct employment with their prospective employer, i.e. the employer where they were located or in legislation known as 'the hirer' (section 13).

The Employment Permits Bill proposes to consolidate existing legislation, to take account of evolving jurisprudence and to cater for future accessions to the EU.

I am concerned about the number of recent cases relating to exploitation of workers. How can this be stopped?
The number of labour inspectors has increased from 31 to 78 (with an additional 12 inspector team managers)

since the end of 2007. Inspectors are specially selected and trained and are deployed on a regional basis. These inspectors can enter premises at a reasonable time, inspect and take records, and interview relevant personnel as required. The inspector's powers are wide-ranging and include enforcement and possible prosecution. For further information, contact 1890 808 090, or check the website www.employmentrights.ie. The onus is on employers to maintain and produce up-to-date statutory records in accordance with legislation.

Payment of Wages

Should my employer provide me with a payslip from my employment?
Yes, under the Payment of Wages Act 1991, your employer must provide you with a written statement of wages and deductions. Section 4 of the Act clearly states that a payslip must show gross wages and an itemised list of deductions. Valid deductions are PAYE, PRSI, pension contributions, etc.

My employer wants to change our payroll from weekly to monthly, and change our payment method from cheque to electronic transfer. Can he do this? Is there any issue of compensation?
Your terms of employment dictate the method and frequency of payment. Your employer must provide you in writing with the changes in your terms of employment (section 5 of the Act). Your employer has up until at least one month after these changes have been implemented to inform you officially in writing. No compensation is due from your employer in relation to these changes, although

it would be advisable for your employer to liaise with you (or your representative) regarding proposed changes (dependent on your company size), and, where possible, provide assistance with such changeover, e.g. "subs", advances or loans. Under section 2 of the Act the employer can pay the employee through any of the following payment methods: cheque, postal/money order, credit transfer or cash, payable at the employer's discretion.

I work for a local authority and have not been a member of a union for over five years. In the Croke Park Agreement the union agreed with the employer to change our payment method from weekly cheque to electronic payment. My employer stopped paying me as I did not give them my bank details for payment by credit transfer. What can I do?

As you are not represented by a union, you are not fundamentally required to comply with the union's agreements made in your absence of representation. It is fundamental your employer comply with all existing employment legislation and normal and existing procedures in place to communicate changes. In this case, the Payment of Wages Act 1991, section 2 clearly sets out the various different acceptable methods of payment, and therefore your employer can pay your wages in any of the methods clearly specified even if you disagree. If your employer refuses to pay you your wages, you can take an action under section 5 of the Payment of Wages Act 1991 for non-payment. It could be argued that as you refused to provide your bank details for payment of your wages through a credit transfer your employer could not pay you, but alternatively it could be argued your employer is in breach of the legislation and payment should remain in place until a hearing/

mediation/conciliation takes place to try to resolve the difficulty.

My employer deducts payments from me for my uniform. Can she do this?
The first thing to consider is whether your terms and conditions of employment clearly state if these deductions are agreed between the parties. Secondly, it must be considered whether such deductions are fair and reasonable in relation to the amount of wages. Thirdly, the employee must be given written notice of deductions at least one week before they are made. It is important to note that under section 8 of the Safety, Health and Welfare at Work Act 2005 employers are obliged to provide Personal Protective Equipment (PPE) free of charge. An employer may not ask for money to be paid to them by an employee for the provision of PPE, whether returnable (e.g. a deposit) or otherwise. Any omissions or deductions of wages must not be made later than six months after the uniform was given to you. A similar case would be if, for example, you work in a shop and your till is short at the end of the day. If your contract allows for deductions from your wages for shortages, your employer cannot deduct the shortage later than six months after it has occurred.

If deductions are to be paid by instalments, the first payment must be made within six months of the date on which the incident occurred (i.e. the date you were given the uniform or your till was short).

In conclusion, it is important to be fully aware of agreed or proposed deductions, e.g. till shortages, breakages and uniforms, and the agreed amounts, methods of payment and the period of time over which deductions will take place. All agreements should be made in advance of such deductions and in writing within your terms of employment, or provided by your employer after consultation and before implementation.

I was overpaid. Am I obliged to declare and repay?
Yes, it would be advisable to declare the overpayment and discuss with your employer how and over what period the payment should be repaid. Section 5(5) of the Payment of Wages Act 1991 allows for excluding the general rule in relation to the six-month window for deduction/overpayment of payments. Therefore, from an employer's perspective, an employer has the right to make any correction in relation to an overpayment (section 5(*a*)(i)(I)) as or when the mistake has been found by the employer. In addition, there is no obligation on an employer to enter arrangements to allow repayments of the overpayment over a period of time in consideration of the employee and the employer can demand the repayment be made in one lump sum.

What if my employer makes deductions without prior notice or warning?
Firstly, it is important to distinguish if an error has been made in good faith or if it was a clerical mistake. Any error should be rectified as quickly as reasonably possible. Secondly, the employee must check whether deductions are determinable as per agreed terms and conditions of employment. Thirdly, the employee must consider whether such deductions exceed the loss or damage sustained by the employer. A disciplinary fine as well as a deduction for such loss or damage may be imposed by the employer, subject to the terms and conditions of employment.

If the deductions do not fall within the confines of the agreements above, it may be found that the employer is in breach of the Payment of Wages Act 1991, and a grievance can be taken through the Workplace Relations Services.

Within what time period can I complain, and can I receive compensation for the inconvenience caused?
A complaint must be made within six months of the unlawful deductions. If, after examination, a hearing shows the complaint is well founded and that the deduction is unlawful, compensation may be awarded to the amount of:

- Net previous weekly wage (prior to deduction)
- If the amount of the deduction is greater than the wage, twice the amount of the deduction

No compensatory payments or interest are chargeable on payments due to an employee from an employer, regardless of the time frame taken to recoup such money.

My employer did not pay me my last week's wages before I left work. What action can I take?
Non-payment of wages or an error in the amount of wages due to an employee will be regarded as an unlawful deduction under the Payment of Wages Act 1991 (unless such error is a miscalculation). The other consideration to determine is whether you complied with the minimum notice requirements prior to leaving your workplace. Therefore, if you have a valid case, an action may be taken through the Workplace Relations Services.

I have been suspended from work without pay pending a hearing. Can my employer do this?
Yes, your employer may be eligible to do this on grounds of their disciplinary procedure. If their procedure allows the company to suspend you without pay and verifies these grounds for suspension without pay, this may be feasible. It is important to note that any hearings or resolutions should take place within a reasonable period of time, in the interests of fair justice.

It is essential, therefore, to have a copy of the company's disciplinary procedure available. Alternatively, recommended best practice guidelines (Code of Practice) in relation to grievance and disciplinary procedures (SI 146/2000) are available from www.lrc.ie.

SUMMARY CHECKLIST: Payment of Wages

Ensure you have checked all the terms and conditions of your ☐ employment regarding agreed deductions or disciplinary procedures.

Ensure you receive a detailed wage slip as appropriate ☐ (weekly, fortnightly, monthly).

Examine the content of your payslip for inaccuracies. Seek ☐ clarification from your employer regarding any inappropriate deductions or miscalculations promptly.

Try to resolve matters with your employer at the time they ☐ occur, before using the structured complaints process (complain through the Workplace Relations Services).

Protection of Young Workers

What restrictions are in place for the number of hours a child can work?
Under the Protection of Young Persons (Employment) Act 1996, section 3(2), restrictions are in place in relation to the

employment of minors. The employer must apply to the Minister at least 21 days before the minor's employment commences. Children under seven years must not be present at the place of work for more than five hours a day (not before 9.30 a.m. or after 4.30 p.m.) or work more than a continuous period of 30 minutes without a total break of two hours or more. Children over seven and under thirteen years must not work for more than seven and a half hours per day (not before 9.00 a.m. or after 5.00 p.m.), or work more than a continuous period of 45 minutes without a total break of three hours or more. Children over thirteen years cannot work for more than eight hours per day (not before 9.00 a.m. or after 7.00 p.m.) or work for more than a period of four hours without a rest (of minimum one hour). Those under sixteen may not be required to work before 8.00 a.m. in the morning or after 8.00 p.m. at night. Other factors taken into consideration by the legislation include the requirement for the child to have a chaperon, educational resources, meal and rest breaks, and travel arrangements.

I am fourteen years old. Can I start paid employment?
Employers are allowed to take on fourteen- and fifteen-year-old children for light work during the school holidays or as part of an approved work experience or education programme (SOLAS (formerly FÁS) or Minister for Jobs, Enterprise and Innovation pre-approved – maximum 40 hours per week). Fourteen-year-old children are not allowed to work during term time (school year), whereas fifteen-year-old children are allowed work up to eight hours per week during term time. The maximum working day is seven hours per day, if the maximum working

week is 35 hours, and eight hours per day, if the maximum working week is 40 hours.

During the summer holidays, children under sixteen must have at least 21 days free from work. Under the Protection of Young Persons (Employment) Act 1996, a child is defined as a person less than sixteen years old, whereas a young person is defined as a person aged sixteen, or who has not yet reached the age of eighteen.

I am sixteen years old and starting work in a bar. Should I receive a contract? Is my employer under any further obligation?
Yes, the employer must provide you with a copy of your terms and conditions of employment. Your employer is also under an additional duty to provide you with a copy of the official summary of the Protection of Young Persons (Employment) Act 1996 within one month (at the latest) of your taking up the position.

My friend (aged seventeen) says he will get a shorter break than me. Is this true?
Children under sixteen receive a longer daily break between working and only have to work four hours to receive their half-hour rest break (see table below).

Rest Breaks	Under 16	16 to Under 18 Years
Half-hour rest break	After 4 hours	After 4½ hours
Daily rest break	14 consecutive hours off	12 consecutive hours off
Weekly rest break	2 days off (consecutive, as far as is practicable)	2 days off (consecutive, as far as is practicable)

My friend is seventeen and is planning to work weekends, but the shop-owner doesn't know until what time he can work.

During school holidays and on weekend nights when the young person has no school the next day, sixteen- and seventeen-year-olds may work up to 10.00 p.m. (11.00 p.m. only by prior ministerial approval). If approved, the morning commencement time is 7.00 a.m.

Are the rules different for part-time work in a bar or licensed restaurant?

Yes, under the Protection of Young Persons (Employment) Act 1996, (Employment in Licensed Premises) Regulations 2001 (SI 350/2001) and (Bar Apprentices) Regulations 2001 (SI 351/2001). These regulations are specifically concerned with young persons (sixteen- or seventeen-year-olds) employed in licensed premises on general duties (general duties do not include the supply of intoxicating liquor for consumption on or off premises) during the summer break, other holidays or as part-time work.

These rules clearly state that young persons may be required to work (at the latest) until 11.00 p.m. (excluding days preceding school days). It is also required that young persons do not recommence work before 7.00 a.m. on the following day. A bar apprentice (sixteen or seventeen years old), in a full-time capacity, may be required to work until midnight on any day and not to begin work before 8.00 a.m. the following day, provided they are supervised by an adult.

I am an employer and wish to take on a fifteen-year-old for work. What responsibilities must I comply with?

As an employer, you must see a copy of their birth certificate or other evidence of age. Children under sixteen must be given written permission from a parent (or guardian) before commencement of employment.

The employer must also keep a full record of every employee under eighteen, containing their name, date of birth, starting and finishing times of work, wage rate and total wage paid. The employer must keep records for at least three years after termination of employment at the place of employment.

The employer must also provide the employee (under eighteen) with a copy of the official summary of the Protection of Young Persons (Employment) Act 1996, together with displaying the summary at the place of work, where it can be easily read.

Ensure you keep comprehensive records of proof of age and working hours on file (for at least three years). Fines of up to €1,904.61 may apply if you are found guilty of an offence and continuous contravention can attract fines of €317.43 per day. Ensure you take additional precautions in relation to the safety, health and welfare of a child or young person at the place of work and take preventative measures.

SUMMARY CHECKLIST: Young Workers

Employees

As a child or young person, be fully aware of the restrictions ☐
on the number of hours you can and cannot work.

Be fully aware of the restrictions on rates of pay, in accord- ☐
ance with the national minimum wage (i.e. if you are under
18 years of age).

Employers

Be aware of the requirements to comply with the regulations ☐
covering:
* Written approval from a parent (or guardian)
* Break times
* National minimum wage and statement requirements (specifically, having copies of the Protection of Young Persons Act visible in the workplace and copies for employees)

Working Hours and Rest Periods

I work 50 hours per week during the summer months. Is my employer allowed to make me do that?
The maximum working week is covered under the Organisation of Working Time Act 1997. The new maximum working week is 48 hours per week. It is important, when analysing your working week, to consider and calculate the average working week over a four- or six-month period. Night workers must be assessed over a two-month period. This may be extended up to twelve months in some situations (where collective registered agreements exist, approved by the Labour Court).

So how do I know what average is relevant to me?
In most cases, the norm is the four-month rule. For work subject to seasonal variation, the six-month rule is applicable. For employees who have collective registered agreements in their sector, the review period can be up to twelve months.

My employer only gives me a 30-minute break for 8 hours worked. Can he do this?
Since March 1998, every employee has a general entitlement to:

- Fifteen minutes break where more than four and a half hours have been worked
- Thirty minutes where more than six hours have been worked (which may include the fifteen-minute break)
- Eleven hours daily rest per 24-hour period
- One period of 24 hours rest per week, following from a daily rest period (eleven hours)
- Shop employees who work between the hours of 11.30 a.m. and 2.30 p.m. must, after six hours, be allowed a break of one hour, which must commence between the hours of 11.30 a.m. and 2.30 p.m. Such breaks may vary by collective registered agreement or customs and practices in your employment sector.

Therefore your employer is correct in granting a minimum of 30 minutes' break for 8 hours worked.

I don't get paid when I am on a break. Can my employer insist that I take a 45-minute or 1-hour break/lunch?
Yes, your employer is not obliged to pay you for your breaks under law and your employer is obliged under law to ensure the minimum breaks are adhered to. An employer can, in their terms and conditions of employment, insist on longer break periods, for which you are not entitled to be paid. The Organisation of Working Time Act 1997 sets down the minimum break periods. Any changes in your breaks would be a change to your terms and conditions of employment, which of course cannot be changed without mutual agreement between employee and employer. An employer cannot provide break periods less than the minimum legislative requirements nor can the employer make payment to employees in lieu of break periods.

I need to take a second job to support my family. My first employer is demanding I take my rest period from my second job, Are they entitled?

In accordance with the Organisation of Working Time Act 1997 an employer may not employ an employee to do any work in a relevant period during which the employee has done work for another employer except where the total of the periods does not exceed the maximum working week of 48 hours as an average over a defined period dependent on their sector of work. In effect, this means that where an employee works for more than one employer the average working week of 48 hours cannot be exceeded. Whenever an employer employs an individual in breach of the above both the employer and the employee shall be guilty of an offence. Therefore, yes, it is important that both employers are aware of other employment by the employee and both employers keep full records of time worked by the employee and ensure at least the minimum breaks/rest periods are complied with (section 15 of the Act).

My employer has provided me with a "zero hour" contract which means that I am not guaranteed any hours work per week. Am I employed or not employed and am I entitled to any pay if I don't work?

Section 18 of the Organisation of Working Time Act 1997 covers "zero" hours contracts and therefore you are employed under a contract of employment. Primarily, this type of employment contracts requires an employee to be available for work for certain hours although not necessarily asked to come in, or as required by an employer. This feature of the legislation also covers situations where, for example, an employee is sent home if things are quiet.

Where an employee suffers a loss by not working hours s/he was requested to work or be available to work, the zero hours provisions of the Act ensure that s/he is compensated for 25 per cent of the time which s/he is required to be available or a maximum of 15 hours' pay, whichever is the lesser.

Therefore, if an employee's contract of employment operates to require the employee to be available for 48 hours in a week, s/he will be entitled to a minimum payment of 12 hours even if not required to work that week, or if an employee is asked to be available to work eight hours and is not called into work s/he will be entitled to a minimum payment of two hours. This has caused conflict with the Department of Social Protection's Jobseekers' schemes with reference to assistance payments as the employee is technically employed to work but has no guarantee of work and this can impinge on the ability of the person to seek a payment under the Jobseekers' schemes if there is no guaranteed work.

I am a member of the Gardaí and work twelve-hour shifts. Does this mean I am entitled to a one-hour break?
Unfortunately the Organisation of Working Time Act 1997 excludes certain types of workers. The following are excluded:

- Members of the Defence Forces
- Members of the Garda Síochána
- The activities of doctors in training (as defined under the European Communities (Organisation of Working Time) (Activities of Doctors in Training) Regulations 2004 (SI 494/2004)
- Transport employees

- Workers at sea
- Family employees (farm or private house) including civil partners

Different arrangements may be in place as agreed under collective registered agreements or according to custom and practice in each sector.

In addition, SI 36/2012 – European Communities (Road Transport) (Organisation of Working Time of Persons Performing Mobile Road Transport Activities) Regulations 2012 sets down a maximum working time of no more than 60 hours per week for a person performing mobile road transport activities and an average of no more than 48 hours per week in a defined reference period. It also states that no person shall work more than six hours without a break of thirty minutes and work no more than nine hours without a forty-five-minute break (including the thirty minutes). The statutory instrument (SI) also sets out restrictions and requirements on night working and obligations on self-employed persons and employers to keep proper records.

The Working Time Directive (Directive 2003/88/EC) sets out the minimum employment conditions in respect of working time, rest breaks and holidays and at present this is being reviewed and may lead to possible further changes through the European Council and the European Parliament in the coming years.

I am a security guard. What are my entitlements for breaks?
The following sectors are excluded under the Organisation of Working Time (General Exemptions) Regulations 1998 (SI 21/1998) and the Organisation of Working Time

84

(Exemptions of Transport Activities) Regulations 1998 (SI 20/1998):

- Transport employees (drivers, etc.)
- Security surveillance (physical presence required)
- Public service (including treatment or care of persons in residential care or institutions)
- Services at a harbour or airport
- Production in the press, radio, television and postal services
- Ambulance, fire and civil protection services
- Production and distribution of gas, water or electricity
- Collection of household refuse
- Industrial activity (cannot by reason be interrupted)
- Agriculture
- Tourism
- Research and development

As a driver, must my employer provide compensatory equivalent rest periods for the breaks I cannot take?
No. Under the Organisation of Working Time (Exemption of Transport Activities) Regulations (SI 20/1998) an employer is not obliged to ensure employees receive equivalent compensatory rest. This may be overruled if it can be found that the employee is not employed wholly or mainly in carrying out the specific duty defined, i.e. driving vehicles (land, air or sea). What this means is that if it can be found that a driver has to carry out other functions (not directly related to driving) as part of his or her role, he or she may be entitled to compensatory rest periods.

Since 23 March 2005, a new EU Road Transport Directive (2002/15/EC) should be implemented in Ireland for mobile workers. Mobile workers are defined as people involved in all road transport activities (driving, loading, work related to safety of vehicles, etc.). The maximum working week should not exceed 48 hours, but can be extended to 60 hours occasionally (must be on average 48 hours over 4 months). Also, the Directive provides an obligation to take a break after six hours of work and an uninterrupted period of eleven hours of rest, and provides that the maximum working day must not, on average, exceed eight hours.

Can I be paid in lieu of rest periods?

No. Employers are not allowed to pay employees in lieu of rest periods in a monetary sense (pay in lieu) or by payment in any other form of material benefit (goods or services). An employer can provide benefits that an employee can gain in a physical environment, and through amenities at work. These may include refreshment facilities, recreational facilities, reading material, alleviation of monotonous work or isolation, or possibly transport to and from work, where and when appropriate.

SUMMARY CHECKLIST: Working Hours and Rest Periods

What sector do you work in, and what is the relevant period of time for the assessment of your average working week (4–12 months dependent on sector)?	☐
Are you entitled to normal break or rest periods?	☐
Are you exempt depending on your job or sector?	☐

Night Working

I work different shifts, e.g. from 6.00 p.m. to 2.00 a.m. and 5.00 a.m. to 1.00 p.m., but my employer will not pay me night shift pay. Can she do this?

Night time is the period between midnight and 7.00 a.m. Night workers are employees who normally work at least three hours of their daily working time during night time. It is also important to note that a night worker must also work at least 50 per cent of their annual number of hours at night.

An employer must also consider maximum working hours where employees work in hazardous conditions (mental or physical). Employees should note the terms and conditions of their employment and any collective registered agreements approved by the Labour Court. Part 6 of the Safety, Health and Welfare (General Application) Regulations 2007 (SI 299/2007) states the steps an employer must take to ensure the health and safety of night workers. Before employing a person to do night work, and at regular intervals while an employee is a night worker, an employer is required to make available an assessment of the effects, if any, on the health of the employee. This assessment must be made available, free of charge, to the employee. Alternatively, if the employee is entitled to have the assessment carried out free of charge (through a medical card or any other private medical cover), the employer must make arrangements to allow the employee to access this entitlement. If a night worker becomes ill as a result of night work, the employer should, whenever possible, assign duties to the employee that do not involve night work and which are suited to that employee (Chapter 3 of the Safety, Health and Welfare (General Application) Regulations 2007 (SI 299/2007), sections 155–157).

If an employee is pregnant and a quarter of her working hours are night work, she may be exempted from doing night work if a doctor certifies it may affect her health and safety and that of her baby. If there is no suitable alternative work she may be given health and safety leave. This also applies for up to 14 weeks after the birth of her child (Chapter 2, sections 148–152).

Therefore, in this situation, your employer is not required to pay night shift pay as you only work two hours within the defined night time period between midnight and 7.00 a.m.

Sunday Working

I work on Sundays. Should I not be paid an additional rate for doing so?
There is a common misconception that employees who work on Sundays are entitled to double time for work completed. It is firstly important to distinguish whether working on a Sunday is part of your normal working week (as per the terms of your contract), and whether your rate of payment includes or excludes a Sunday rate premium. It is also important to ensure that rates of pay for overtime (if applicable) or weekend and/or Sunday rates are clearly detailed in your terms and conditions of employment. Therefore, your rate of pay (if part of your normal working hours) may include an additional premium for Sunday work. If not included, employees are entitled to an additional supplement for Sundays, which should be equivalent to the closest collective registered agreement in your sector. The additional Sunday rate premium therefore is not pre-defined in legislation, but must be 'greater than' your normal working rate of pay. A premium may be in the form of additional pay, time off in lieu, portion of shift premium or an unsociable hours premium.

Overtime

I believe it's time-and-a-half rate for Saturday and double time for Sunday. Is this correct?
No, this is not automatically correct. In general, there is no legislation covering overtime. Employees do not have a statutory entitlement to overtime pay. Policy on overtime must be clearly stated in your terms and conditions of employment or as defined through collective registered agreements across sectors.

Employees are entitled to an additional supplement for Sundays, which should be equivalent to the closest collective registered agreement in your sector. This additional supplement may or may not be already incorporated into your rate of pay (if part of your normal working hours).

A premium (overtime) may be in the form of additional pay, time off in lieu, portion of shift premium or an unsociable hours premium. It is therefore advisable to seek clarification on overtime rates as part of your terms of employment or with your employer prior to the commencement of such (additional) work.

Sick Pay and Sick Leave

What is the difference between certified and uncertified sick leave?
Uncertified sick leave is when your employer does not require you to provide medical proof that you were unable to come to work. Certified sick leave is when your employer requires you to provide medical proof that you were unable to work due to illness.

What are my entitlements for sick leave?

There is no legislation obliging employers to provide paid sick benefit to employees. There is an obligation on an employer to provide, in your written terms and conditions of employment, their policy on sick leave and payment.

Does my employer pay me while on sick leave?

Your employer is only obliged to pay you for sick leave if this term is clearly stated in your terms and conditions of employment or through collective registered agreements. If an employer states in their terms and conditions of employment that sick leave is paid and they refuse to pay you for sick leave, you may then have a cause for action under the Payment of Wages Act 1991, for non-payment of wages. Alternatively, if your employer pays other colleagues "sick pay" but not you, you may have a case for discrimination (under the nine grounds – Employment Equality Act 1998, discussed below). If an employer decides to change his or her policy on (paid) sick leave, it would be advisable for him or her to inform all employees of such change (as previously mentioned in the section on terms of employment) in advance of the change, and reinforce it in writing.

What happens if I am sick during my annual leave entitlement?

Any certified sickness during your annual leave should be notified to your employer as soon as possible and therefore any annual leave utilised during the certified sickness may be returned to you at a later date by agreement with your employer. Annual leave cannot be used to cover certified or uncertified sickness.

I went home sick from my job at 11.00 a.m. (8.30 a.m. start) one day last week. Do I get paid for the full day or a half day?
This issue is purely at the discretion of your employer. The policy on sick leave must be clearly stated in your terms and conditions of employment and/or the employee handbook (if applicable). Custom and practice and possible collective registered agreements in your sector of employment are also factors to consider.

I could not make it to work today because of the weather conditions. What is the situation regarding my pay?
There is no legislation specifically within this area, and any decision is purely at the discretion of your employer. Your employer may deduct pay on the grounds of your unscheduled absence from work. Your employer may accept a "sick note" if you are medically unfit for work (subject to your terms and conditions of employment), or your employer may pay you in full. An employer is only under an obligation to your health and safety, both physical and mental, within the confines of your place of work (discussed below).

How can I claim sick pay?
There are two ways of claiming sick pay:

- If clearly stated by your employer under your terms and conditions of employment, your employer will comply with the provision of sick pay, as long as such leave is within a defined period during the calendar year. The administration of such a system may vary from company to company and may involve each employee claiming benefit from the Department of Social Protection and/or reimbursing the organisation with such benefit.

* The employee, if no such scheme exists within their company, may seek to claim Illness Benefit from the Department of Social Protection (if applicable). The employee must complete a form, available from their GP, and forward it as soon as possible. Employees generally do not receive payment for the first three days (known as "waiting days") from the Department of Social Protection.

From 2014 there will be changes to the existing "sick" arrangements for employees in the public sector as follows (announced in July 2012 as part of the Labour Court hearing under clause 1.24 of the Public Service Agreement 2010–2014):

* Certified sick leave – reduced to three months' full pay (from six months) and three months' half pay (from six months) followed by a basic "temporary rehabilitative" payment with a reasonable prospect of return to work, (rate subject to years of service tapering off in line with the existing State Illness Benefit Scheme) for up to a further eighteen months (previously unlimited)
* Critical illness – no change to existing arrangements, i.e. six months' full pay and six months' half pay. Critical illness can be defined as "an exceptional and normally non-recurring occurrence".
* Uncertified sick leave – reduced to seven days in a two-year rolling period (from seven days in a twelve-month period)

In Budget 2013 the Minister for Education and Skills announced that schools will be required to refer teachers and special needs assistants (SNAs) to the occupational health service (similar to a company doctor) after four weeks of sick leave (previously twelve weeks for teachers and eight weeks for SNAs). In addition, the Minister announced that from 1 May 2013 paid absence days (in lieu of days during the maternity leave period when schools are closed) will be removed. These paid absences were previously up to a maximum of 30 days. This change will not affect teachers/SNAs entitled to full maternity leave (26 weeks) and the optional 16 weeks' unpaid maternity leave under existing maternity legislation.

There are also proposals to reduce the liability of cost to employers to pay the first three days of sickness in the public sector, thus in turn, the employee being responsible for their own costs. In addition, there are proposals for employers, both public and private sector, (rather than the State) to be responsible for payment of "sick pay" for the period between two and six months, dependent on the size of the employer. These proposals will require legislative change before implementation.

SUMMARY CHECKLIST: Shift, Sunday, Overtime and Sick Pay

Night Working: do you work at least three hours and half your normal annual hours at night (between midnight and 7.00 a.m.)? If so, you appear to be entitled to night shift pay. □

Sunday Working: check your contract to see if your rate for Sunday working includes a premium rate or not. If not, clarify what the exact rate is. □

Overtime: clarify the rates of pay for overtime with your employer/sector of employment. □

Sick Pay/Leave: clarify (in your terms of contract) your employer's sick pay/leave policy, and the procedure to be administered. □

Public Holidays

What are my entitlements for public holidays?
There are nine public holidays per year. These are as follows:

- News Year's Day (1 January)
- St Patrick's Day (17 March)
- Easter Monday
- First Monday in May
- First Monday in June
- First Monday in August
- Last Monday in October
- Christmas Day (25 December)
- St Stephen's Day (26 December)

Also, as qualifying criteria, part-time employees must have worked forty hours in the previous five weeks (ending the day before the public holiday) to qualify for the public holiday (full-time employees have nearly always automatic entitlement).

Therefore, the Act shows that part-time employees working eight hours or more per week are eligible for public holiday pay if they complete forty hours in the previous five weeks.

The entitlements for employees in respect of public holidays are whichever of the following their employer determines:

- A paid day off on the day in question (public holiday)
- A paid day off within a month of such day
- An additional day of annual leave
- An additional day's pay

Example 1

Mary works four days a week (Monday–Thursday), four hours per day as a cleaner (sixteen hours per week). She wishes to calculate her public holiday entitlement.

Mary would have worked sixteen hours per week for the five-week period prior to the public holiday (eighty hours). Therefore she is eligible under the forty-hour eligibility rule.

Because Mary normally works on Monday, the following criteria may apply:

- If the business is closed on the day in question, Mary is entitled to be paid for the day and receive the day off.
- If the business is open on the day in question, Mary receives her normal day's pay and any one of the following:
  - An additional day's pay for work completed (normal daily rate last worked)
  - An additional paid day's leave within a month of the day
  - An additional paid day of annual leave

The employer must nominate in advance which option will be implemented.

Example 2

Joan works two days a week (Tuesday and Wednesday), three hours per day as a retail assistant (six hours per week). She wishes to calculate her public holiday entitlement.

Unfortunately, Joan is not entitled to the public holiday benefit, as she has not worked forty hours in the previous five weeks.

Example 3

Sheila works three days a week (Wednesday to Friday), five hours per day as a hairdresser (fifteen hours per week). She wishes to calculate her public holiday entitlement.

Sheila is entitled to the public holiday benefit, as she has worked 75 hours in the previous 5 weeks. Therefore she is eligible under the 40-hour eligibility rule.

Because Sheila does not normally work on Monday, the following criteria may apply:

- Sheila is entitled to one-fifth additional pay (regardless of the number of days of the week she works) of her normal week's pay, or
- The equivalent paid time off (one-fifth of her working week) within a month of the day, or
- Additional paid time (one-fifth of her normal week) in annual leave

The employer must nominate in advance which option will be implemented.

What happens if I am sick prior to a public holiday; am I still entitled to the paid leave?

If you are a part-time employee, such eligibility to the public holiday would be determined by the normal rule of having worked 40 hours in the previous 5 weeks (from the date prior to the pending public holiday). If you meet the criteria, you are eligible for the entitlement to a public holiday.

If you are a full-time employee, you are entitled to the public holiday entitlement if you are off sick, subject to you not having exhausted a maximum of 26 weeks off sick (ordinary illness) or a maximum of 52 weeks, if it was an occupational injury (injury at work), prior to the pending public holiday. Such entitlement may be in addition to any sick pay scheme from your employer or granted by the Department of Social Protection under the Illness Benefit Scheme (presuming your illness is not within the three-day 'waiting' period at the commencement of your claim).

What is the situation regarding Good Friday? Is it a public holiday?

Good Friday, Christmas Eve and New Year's Eve are bank holidays (when banks are closed) and not public holidays, i.e. statutory entitlements, although the Minister has the power by regulation to nominate any additional days as public holidays. In 1999, the Minister approved New Year's Eve as a one-off special public holiday in celebration of the Millennium.

Therefore, the above days are normal working days and subject to the normal annual leave requirements. Some organisations, through terms and conditions of employment, customs and practice, and collective registered agreements may facilitate the above days as discretionary paid leave.

What is the situation if a public holiday falls on a weekend?

If a public holiday falls on a weekend, generally the benefits are automatically transferred to the next weekday. Therefore, with regard to St Patrick's Day in 2012 (17 March 2012) as it fell on a Saturday (and most people were already off) the benefit was moved to the Monday (19 March 2012). In this case, Monday 19 March 2012 did not become a public holiday; the benefit (as a norm) is simply transferred to the Monday for employees who do not work at weekends. In other cases (employees who work weekends), arrangements must be made in advance by employers as to how public holiday entitlements will be facilitated.

How do I know whether or not I have to work on a public holiday?

An employee may, at least 21 days prior to the public holiday, request their employer to clarify the situation regarding the forthcoming public holiday. The employee must be notified of the employer's decision at least fourteen days before the public holiday. If the employer fails to comply with the request from the employee, the employee shall be entitled to a paid day's leave for the proposed day.

What rate of pay do I receive for the public holiday?

Firstly, the agreement regarding arrangements for working on a public holiday must be set down by your employer (if above the minimum statutory entitlement). As mentioned above, the agreement may state one of the following:

- An additional day's pay – this will mean, in summary, double time, i.e. your normal daily rate and an additional day's pay.
- The daily rate of pay is calculated to be the amount that was paid to the employee on the last working day prior to the public holiday, i.e. if the public holiday falls on Monday, and your normal working week is Monday–Friday, the daily rate paid on the last working day before the public holiday is the rate paid on the previous Friday.

- An additional day's paid leave within a month – in this situation you will be paid your daily rate (single rate) as normal and you will be granted an additional day of paid leave to be used within one month.
- An additional day of paid (annual) leave – in this situation you will be paid your daily rate (single rate) as normal. The additional day will be added to your normal leave entitlement, to be used within the agreed policy of the company regarding scheduled leave.

Some employers pay additional rates of payment over and above the minimum entitlement (as stated above). This is at the discretion of your employer.

It is advisable to be fully aware of the arrangements for each public holiday in advance of the agreement to work on a public holiday.

I job-share with my colleague. What is the proper calculation for public holiday leave pay?
Before calculating such a rate, there are three key assumptions:

- Neither employee generally works on a public holiday.
- Job-share employees work half the time of full-time employees.
- Pay is calculated within a fixed rate or salary.

If this is the case, the rate of pay for public holidays will be one-tenth of the normal rate of pay over the two weeks prior to the public holiday. It is important to note that such rate of pay should not be greater than half a normal day's pay.

I am finishing work with the company this Friday before the public holiday. Am I still entitled to be paid for the public holiday?
Yes, as long as the employee meets the criterion of 40 hours worked in the previous 5 weeks, the employee will be entitled to be paid on departure from such employment.

I am on maternity leave. Am I still entitled to the public holiday leave entitlement?
Employees on maternity, parental and adoptive leave are still entitled to public holiday pay. Such employees are classified as being in continuous employment during planned leave and, therefore, are still entitled to agreed terms.

SUMMARY CHECKLIST: Public Holidays

Are you a full-time or part-time worker? If part-time, have you ☐
worked 40 hours in the previous 5 weeks? If so, you are
entitled to paid public holiday leave entitlement.

Have you been sick, and for how long prior to the public ☐
holiday?

What is your employer's policy for Good Friday? Does the ☐
employer provide any discretionary paid leave entitlement?

Has your employer complied with the notice period in ☐
advance of the public holiday?

Are you working or not, and what is the rate of pay? ☐

Are you ever scheduled to work on a public holiday? If not, ☐
you should not lose out on the entitlement (one-fifth of your
working week's pay).

Do you job-share (and meet the requirements) (one-tenth ☐
working week pay due)?

How long have you worked for the company? ☐

Are you on maternity, parental or adoptive leave? If so, your ☐
public holiday entitlements are protected.

Holiday Entitlements

What are my entitlements for annual leave?
Under the Organisation of Working Time Act 1997, an employee's minimum leave entitlement is one of the following:

- Four working weeks in a leave year (subject to completing 1,365 hours)
- One-third of a working week per calendar month (subject to 117 hours worked)
- Eight per cent of hours worked in a leave year (subject to a maximum of four weeks)

Example

Mary works four days a week, four hours per day as a cleaner (sixteen hours per week). She wishes to calculate her annual leave.

Option 1

Mary receives four working weeks in a leave year.
4 weeks × 16 hours per week = 64 hours

Option 2

One-third of a working week per calendar month:
Of 4 days per week = 1 1/3 days × 12 months = 16 days (4 weeks)

Option 3

8 per cent of hours worked:
16 hours per week × 52 weeks = 832 hours

8 per cent of 832 hours = 66.56 hours
66.56 hours ÷ 16 hours per week = 4.16 weeks (4 weeks).

As we can see from the above calculations, whichever method you use, the outcome is generally the same, i.e. four working weeks (the minimum provision under the Act). Employers may, at their discretion (as per collective registered agreements or terms and conditions of employment), grant additional paid leave over and above the statutory minimum.

Do my holiday entitlements include the public holidays?

Your holiday entitlements are in addition to the public holiday leave entitlement. Therefore, total paid leave (for someone working Monday–Friday) can be (at minimum) as much as 29 days (20 days leave (4 weeks) and 9 public holidays) if or where applicable.

How do I calculate my holiday pay?

Holiday pay is generally calculated as the normal working weekly or monthly rate last worked by the employee before their planned leave (salary rate). This rate should include any regular bonus or allowances paid which are not dependent on work done and exclude any pay for overtime.

Alternatively, if the weekly rate is calculated by productivity or commission, the weekly rate may be calculated as being the average weekly rate of pay over the thirteen weeks prior to commencing holiday leave (excluding overtime).

I was sick over the last two weeks and I work on commission. What will my rate of holiday pay be for my leave next week?
The rate of pay will be the average rate of pay over the previous thirteen weeks worked. The thirteen-week period ends on the last day worked by the employee. Therefore, in this case, it will be the average of the thirteen-week period starting fifteen weeks ago, i.e. the period prior to sickness.

What hours do I include or exclude in calculating my holiday leave?

Include	Exclude
All hours worked	Sick leave
Maternity leave	Occupational injury leave
Parental leave	Temporary lay-off
First 13 weeks of carer's leave	Career break
Force majeure leave	

Do I lose my entitlement to holiday leave if I am sick?
In general, no, but this may vary depending on the length of time you are sick over the calendar year.

As holiday leave is calculated in relation to hours worked, it is essential to meet and achieve a key 'marker' in relation to the number of hours worked, i.e. 1,365 hours per year or 117 hours per month.

If we were to assess a normal employee working 39 hours per week, they would achieve the 1,365 hours within 35 weeks. Therefore, the employee would have to be sick for more than 17 weeks (of a total of 52) to lose holiday entitlements.

In the monthly example, similarly an employee working 39 hours per week would achieve the holiday entitlements within 3 working weeks per month. The European Court of Justice (ECJ) has held that workers do not lose the right to paid annual leave which they have been unable to take because of illness (Joined Cases C-350/06 and C-520/06). The right to paid annual leave is contained in the Working Time Directive (Directive 2003/88/EC).

I wish to take the first two weeks off in August, but my employer will not allow me. Can he do this?
Yes. The employer decides when holiday leave can or cannot be taken. It would be advisable for employers to consider work–life balance, rest and recreation, and planning of leave during the calendar year, but the employee must also consider peak operational or seasonal periods. It would be advisable for employees to consult with their employers and plan scheduled leave during the agreed calendar period.

I am currently on carer's leave; will my holiday entitlement be affected?
Annual leave is not affected by other leave provided for by law. Time spent on adoptive leave, parental leave, force majeure leave and the first thirteen weeks of carer's leave is treated as though you have been in employment and this time can be used to accumulate annual leave entitlements.

I am going on holidays next week, but my employer has not informed me if I will be paid in advance.

Holiday pay should be paid in advance at the normal weekly rate.

I don't have any holidays planned. Can I ask my employer to pay me in lieu of my leave?
No. Your employer is not allowed to pay you in lieu of your holiday leave, except in circumstances where your employment has ceased with your current employer.

I don't normally take two weeks leave at any one time, but my employer is forcing me to do so. Can she do that?
After eight months of work, an employee is entitled to two weeks' unbroken leave, which may include one or more public holidays, although this is not enforceable by the employer unless a collective registered agreement or the terms and conditions of employment stipulate such an arrangement.

In December every year I have an argument with my employer regarding leave I have left for the year. I want to carry them forward, but he won't allow me. Who is right?
The official calendar year under the legislation is 1 April–31 March, although many employers comply with the normal calendar year. It is advisable to plan or schedule leave over the twelve-month period. This is advisable from the employer's perspective, to take into account busy periods (when leave is not possible) and to ensure compliance with recommendations for a work–life balance. It is also advisable from the employee's perspective to take into consideration the procedure for applying for leave within the company, i.e. how many employees can take leave at any one time, balancing leave over the twelve months and taking into account when leave may not be possible, all of

which may lead to employees having to take leave when they may not wish to take it. Order of preference for leave may be dependent on seniority, or leave may be restricted due to peak business periods. These factors affect both the employer and the employee, and should be planned collaboratively.

Another factor, which must be considered, is the policy of the company in relation to the carrying over of leave, i.e. if the company allow such practices and to what extent. Holiday leave may be extended, with prior agreement, to be used within the first six-month period of the following year. It would be advisable for the employer to ensure each employee avails of at least their statutory minimum leave (four weeks) during the leave year. Therefore the company should have a clear and fully informed policy on the carry-over of leave.

Any dispute between employer and employee is one that can only be resolved locally, unless the employee did not (through valid reasons) avail of their minimum statutory leave, i.e. four weeks within the leave year. If the employee did not avail of, or was not permitted to take, all his/her minimum statutory leave (four weeks) within the twelve-month period, or if no agreement can be reached in relation to the 'carry-over' of annual leave, it may be advisable to seek intervention from the Workplace Relations Services through either mediation, conciliation or the complaints procedure (www.workplacerelations. ie).

What if I have a dispute with my employer regarding leave used? What can I do?
Your employer must keep records for a period of three years per employee for inspection and investigation. This

is enforced under the Organisation of Working Time (Records) (Prescribed Form and Exemptions) Regulations 2001, which requires an employer to keep detailed records of employment, including start and end times, working days and working weeks, as well as leave granted.

SUMMARY CHECKLIST: Holiday Entitlements

Does your contract state what your annual leave entitlement is? ☐

What are the arrangements for booking annual leave within your company? Are there any restrictions? ☐

Which method does your employer use to calculate your annual leave entitlement? ☐

Are you paid your holiday pay in advance? ☐

Do you work part-time? Keep a note of your total hours worked (8 per cent of hours worked – maximum 4 working weeks). ☐

How is your holiday pay calculated (flat rate salary/commission)? You may need to calculate your average over the previous thirteen weeks worked. ☐

Were you sick or absent from work during the year? ☐

Are the hours "reckonable", i.e. included or excluded when calculating annual leave? (See table on p. 103.) ☐

What is the policy of your company in relation to the carry-over of leave to the following year? ☐

Safety and Welfare at Work

What are my employer's duties regarding my safety at work?

The Safety, Health and Welfare at Work Act 1989 imposes a general duty on each employer to provide a safe place of work, a planned system of work, information, training, consultation and emergency plans in relation to safety.

This also includes non-employees and the self-employed. The Safety and Welfare at Work Act 2005 contains additional requirements to prevent improper conduct or behaviour affecting employees (e.g. bullying and sexual harassment) and requires the appointment of persons in the organisation as safety officers.

As an employee, do I have any duties to my boss?

Yes. The 1989 Act imposes a general duty to take reasonable care at work for your safety and that of your colleagues. It also provides a duty to use all protective clothing, use equipment properly and report promptly any situation that may cause injury to someone. It is advisable for employees to consult with their employers regarding safety issues and representation to ensure collective involvement regarding health and safety at work.

What is a 'safety statement' and what should be in it? Should I be informed?

A safety statement is a document in writing covering safety at work, identification of risks and steps to minimise or remove such risks where appropriate. Each employee should be aware of the statement and its impact on the work environment.

I have heard my employer will have the right to breathalyse me before I start work. Will this be possible?

Under the Safety, Health and Welfare at Work Act 2005, an employee has a duty to ensure they are not under the influence of alcohol or drugs in the workplace. This additional requirement allows employers to ensure employees are not intoxicated before or during working hours. This may allow employers to implement random testing in the workplace and certain disciplinary procedures may (if stated in the terms of employment or disciplinary procedure) be imposed.

Can my employer force me to be medically assessed?
Yes. Under the Safety, Health and Welfare at Work Act 2005, employees are required to undergo any reasonable medical or other assessment if requested by the employer.

Assessments may be required on the grounds of medical examination (prior to your commencement of employment), verification of the seriousness of an illness or to assess that the employee is not under the influence of alcohol or drugs and putting themselves or their colleagues at risk. Periodic medical assessments may also be necessary on the grounds of the nature of the work and risk implications, especially for night workers.

In all cases, the grounds for medical assessment by the employer must be reasonable and the employee can gain access to such information stored by or on behalf of the employer unless such disclosure would cause them harm either physically or mentally.

For further information contact the Health and Safety Authority at 01-6147010 or check www.hsa.ie.

SUMMARY CHECKLIST: Safety and Welfare at Work

Have you access to or have you seen the company's safety statement? ☐

Are you aware of risks to safety in your workplace, and have you reported them to your employer? ☐

Are you intoxicated at work? What are the implications for you, your colleagues or the public of such risks? ☐

Are there any medical implications you should inform your employer about? ☐

Privacy at Work

I suspect that my employer has installed CCTV cameras on the premises, especially in the staff room. Is this legal? What can I do about it?
If you believe your employer has installed CCTV cameras on the premises, especially in the staff room, firstly it would be advisable to consult with your employer to verify if this is true or not. Your employer can install CCTV systems in the workplace, but generally it is best to consult with employees before and during installation. The employer should also consult with employees regarding the procedures for using and storing data in compliance with data protection legislation (Data Protection Acts 1998–2003). The level of surveillance must have just cause and be necessary, fair and reasonable, and in the interests of both the employer and employee.

Regardless of any allegations by the employer (even in the light of proof by CCTV), the employer must ensure that he or she complies with the disciplinary procedure of the company, including a fair and reasonable right to appeal by the employee. The sayings *audi alteram partum* ('the right to be heard') and *nemo judex in sua causa* ('a person should not be judge in their own cause' – the rule against bias) are rules of natural justice and are especially relevant to employers with regard to the implementation of disciplinary procedures. The incorrect carrying out of disciplinary procedures by the employer may open the door for an employee to contest any such dismissal as 'unfair'. In summary, it is advisable to discuss your concerns with your employer regarding the implications and purpose of such surveillance (if feasible to do so, unless the Gardaí have a criminal investigation underway), the issue of data protection and the issue of fair and reasonable surveillance, in the interests of both employer and employee. Hidden surveillance may be feasible without the employees' consent in cases of criminal investigation by the Gardaí, as long as such surveillance is fair and reasonable.

Can my employer monitor my e-mail, internet and telephone usage in the workplace?
Yes, employers can monitor usage of such services in the workplace, subject to a number of conditions. Employees should be informed in their contract of employment or staff handbook of the rules regarding the usage of equipment. An agreement may also be of a verbal nature.

The policy should clearly state if personal use of such equipment is allowed during working hours and the implications of inappropriate usage or that which causes offence to others in the workplace. Inappropriate usage must not be in breach of any equality legislation, or breach the bullying, harassment or sexual harassment policies of the company. Breaches may be classified as serious disciplinary issues.

The legal reason for telephone announcements saying "calls are being recorded for quality and training purposes" is to notify or warn the public that a recording is being made and may be reused.

Can my employer ask to look at my Facebook account? I updated my Facebook account during work hours, can I be disciplined? What if I put comments on my Facebook account when I was meant to be in work?
There are a number of factors to consider. It is important to be aware, in the terms and conditions of employment, if there are any clauses in relation to the potential

impact of your actions on the image of the company and if, in the contract, the employer can proceed with disciplinary action if any action of the employee impinges on the company image/brand. Therefore, an employee must be careful of their actions outside the work environment and the potential impact on their employer. These include actions/comments on social networking sites of which you have direct control and/or articles in newspapers, magazines or online, i.e. court cases, criminal activity, etc.

In answer to the question, an employer cannot ask to access your Facebook account directly, but if it is an open account obviously it can be accessed by any member of the public and, as such, any relevant information which may impact on the employer and their organisation can be used in evidence for disciplinary purposes if required.

In addition, in your contract there should be a clear policy in relation to use of ICT (information and communications technology) equipment during working hours. This includes all equipment used or supplied by the employer, e.g. mobile phones, PCs, laptops and iPads. The ICT policy should set down clearly misuse of such equipment and the possible implications for the employee. Some employers may have the ability to restrict access to certain sites within their workplace, or be able to monitor use of certain sites by each employee. Therefore, if employees use ICT material for personal use during work time it is both affecting productivity, i.e. not doing your work, and is possibly in breach of the ICT policy. Many employers, as stated, can monitor and access material accessed by an employee on social network sites within their workplace and this evidence can or could be used for disciplinary purposes.

Can I access my files at work? Who has the right to access my files (other than my employer) and what can be done if the files are incorrect?
All employees can have access to their personal work files (under data protection legislation).

Generally, your employer restricts third-party access to your files, subject to exceptions, which include the Gardaí and Revenue, who can have access to your files without your consent. The Department of Social Protection is excluded from accessing your files without your consent.

If you find information on your files to be incorrect, you are entitled to have the information corrected.

SUMMARY CHECKLIST: Privacy at Work	
Have you been consulted by your employer of potential CCTV monitoring?	☐
Is there a valid reason why CCTV monitoring should be in place?	☐
What is the company policy on CCTV, internet and telephone usage and monitoring, and data storage, and what are the disciplinary implications of abuse of resources?	☐

Discrimination, Bullying, Stress and Harassment

I went for an interview recently. I felt some of the questions were inappropriate. How do I know if I was discriminated against? And what can I do about it?
Discrimination may be direct, indirect or by association. Discrimination is defined under the Employment Equality Acts 1998–2004 as the treatment of a person in a less favourable way than another person is, has been or would be treated in a comparable situation on any of the following nine grounds:

- Gender
- Civil status (marital/civil partnership status)
- Family status
- Sexual orientation
- Religion
- Age
- Disability
- Race
- Membership of the Traveller community

If you feel discrimination took place through inappropriate questions, in relation to your circumstances or in relation to the specific grounds mentioned above, it would be advisable to seek clarification regarding your complaint from the company in writing. The company's reply may affect the outcome of a complaint if taken to the Workplace Relations Services. Complaints regarding discrimination can be invalid where the following is in question:

- A person's capacity and competence in his or her job (ability to undertake duties)
- A person's educational, technical or professional qualifications (certain standards apply)
- Eligibility criteria and positive discrimination in relation to pregnancy, religion and disability

A complaint can be made to the Workplace Relations Services within six months of the date of the last act of discrimination (under the nine grounds). Workplace Relations can recommend mediation (with the consent of the parties) or formal investigation.

Positive outcomes may include compensation, equal treatment or redeployment.

I feel I have been discriminated against during my employment by my colleague. Who is responsible, my colleague or the company?

Employers are vicariously responsible, i.e. responsible for anything done by the employee in the course of employment, unless the employer can prove they took reasonable steps to prevent such discrimination.

Some employers may have anti-discrimination policies or training in place to prevent such actions, thereby restricting possible liability in cases of discrimination.

It may be advisable to make your complaint informally to the individual (depending on the severity of the issue) or formally to the employer (through normal protocol). The employer, ideally, should have a clear grievance procedure stating defined steps and time frames for dealing with such a complaint (see Code of Practice in Relation to Grievance and Disciplinary Procedures – SI 146/2000). If the company pleads ignorance or their response is unacceptable, the complainant (the person making the complaint) can make a complaint to the Workplace Relations Services within six months of the date of the last act of discrimination (under the nine grounds). Workplace Relations can recommend mediation (with the consent of parties) or formal investigation.

Positive outcomes may include compensation, equal treatment or redeployment. Frivolous claims to the Workplace Relations Services may be struck out after one year if such cases are unsubstantiated.

I am concerned that, if I take a case, my employer will target me. Can she do that?

No. It is unlawful for an employer to victimise an employee for taking an action under the Employment

Equality Acts. An employer must not victimise the claimant for taking an action, or for informing their employer of a claim they made, or supporting a colleague who made a complaint.

I think I am being bullied but I am not sure if my employer was just having a 'bad day'. What should I do?
Bullying essentially is repeated aggression, verbal, psychological or physical, by an individual or group against another person. Isolated acts of aggression are not, therefore, defined as bullying. As we can all understand, each employee has various personal traits, interpersonal skills, work pressures and life pressures, as well as environmental work factors impinging on his or her day-to-day life. This is the normal mix in any workplace.

The essential elements to look for in relation to bullying are repeated aggression, cruelty, viciousness, intimidation and dominance regarding the working relationship. As we have seen, the employer has a duty of care for the safety, health and welfare of all employees, not just physically, but also psychologically.

Recommended codes of practice (SI 17/2002) are available for employers to address bullying in the workplace. An employer can take pro-active, positive steps to remove future liabilities in this vein. Complaints may be taken to the Workplace Relations Services under the Safety, Health and Welfare at Work Act 2005.

What is the difference between harassment and sexual harassment?
Harassment is any form of unwanted conduct towards a person relating to the nine grounds outlined in the Employment Equality Acts 1998–2004.

Sexual harassment is any form of unwanted verbal, non-verbal or physical conduct of a sexual nature. Harassment, sexual or otherwise, may include acts, requests, spoken words, gestures, and displays of words, pictures or material. It is conduct that affects a person's dignity and creates an intimidating, hostile or offensive environment for the person to work in. Harassment of an employee may occur via another employee, the employer or any third party in a working relationship with the organisation. As we have seen above, the employer is vicariously liable for such harassment, unless they have taken appropriate and reasonable practical steps to prevent or eliminate it from taking place. Codes of practice are available for employers in relation to sexual harassment and harassment at work (Employment Equality Act 1998 (Code of Practice) (Harassment) Order 2002 (SI 78/2002)).

What is the procedure for dealing with bullying or harassment at work?

In relation to an individual complaint, it would be advisable to keep a diary of such events for future reference. If possible, approach the perceived bully or harasser, informing them that their actions are inappropriate (without antagonism). In many cases the perceived bully or harasser may not be aware of the effects of their actions. Another option would be to bring the complaint to your employer. Such problems can sometimes be resolved informally through dialogue or mediation. Alternatively, the complaint may have to be processed through the company's grievance procedure for formal investigation and resolution. Corrective action may be taken to restrict future work contact (where feasible), training may be provided for the perceived bully or harasser or, in some cases, disciplinary action may be taken, depending on the seriousness of the complaint. If the employer does not take reasonable steps to remedy or alleviate the situation, the complainant may seek intervention through the Workplace Relations Services under the Safety, Health and Welfare at Work Act 2005 and the Industrial Relations Acts 1969–2012. Alternatively, the employee may feel they are forced to leave due to the work environment, and would then be eligible to pursue an action for constructive dismissal. In May 2007 a new Code of Practice for Employers and Employees on the Prevention and Resolution of Bullying at Work was implemented. The new code incorporates the provision of the Safety, Health and Welfare Act 2005 to prevent improper conduct or behaviour at work. It recommends the identification of possible risks of bullying in the workplace, and the reinforcement of clear internal informal processes and procedures (including mediation) to assist in resolving bullying disputes.

The European social partners (trade unions and employer organisations) have signed a framework agreement on harassment and violence at work. The agreement aims to prevent and manage problems with bullying, sexual harassment and physical violence at work.

My workload is getting too much for me. I have had to take time off work because of this. What should I do?
Generally, stress is the feeling of distress and not coping emotionally or psychologically with excess workloads and demands in relation to a person's capacity.

As we have mentioned, an employer has a duty of care for your safety, health and welfare at work, both physical and mental. You should inform your employer that your workload is leading to stress and perhaps stress-related illness.

The employer, having been made aware of this, should take all reasonable steps to remedy the situation through workload management, assessment of the employee's capacity and assessment of his or her needs and supports. If the employer does not take reasonable steps to remedy or alleviate the situation within a reasonable period of time, the employee may be in a position to claim for constructive dismissal and/or civil action (on grounds of negligence).

SUMMARY CHECKLIST: Discrimination, Bullying, Stress and Harassment

Have you been treated less than favourably under any of the nine grounds?	☐
Are the actions of a colleague inappropriate and do they cause personal anguish?	☐
Has the company incorporated recommended codes of practice and what is its policy? What steps should be taken?	☐
Have you kept a log of events? Have you informed your employer?	☐
What steps has the employer taken to rectify the situation?	☐
What are the triggers causing stress? What can be done to reduce the risk (if any)?	☐
Are there safety and welfare at work implications?	☐

CHAPTER 2

Additional Employment Rights

Jury Duty

I have been called for jury duty but my employer will not allow me to attend. What can I do?
It is an employer's duty to allow an employee to attend jury duty. However, an employer may be excused from allowing their employee to fulfil such duty on the grounds of "good reason" as clearly laid out in writing by the employer and if approved by the County Registrar. The following are disqualified from jury service:

- Non-Irish citizens residing in Ireland
- People convicted of a serious offence and imprisoned for three months or more in the last ten years or imprisoned at any stage for five years or more

The following may also be excluded from jury duty:

- People working in 'essential' services – doctors, nurses, etc.
- Those who served on a jury in the last three years, or who have been excused by a judge

- Full-time students
- Members of religious orders
- Members of the Oireachtas (including staff and civil servants)
- Local authority and HSE staff
- School teachers and university lecturers

There is no upper age limit since 1 January 2009 under the Civil Law (Miscellaneous Provisions) Act 2008 (Commencement) Order 2008, SI 274/2008.

Do I still get paid when on jury duty?

Yes, an employee is entitled to pay while on jury duty, as per the Juries Act 1976. Those who are self-employed and working alone may qualify for an exclusion from jury service on the grounds that it may affect their ability to earn a living.

The court released me from duty this morning at 11.30 a.m. Can I go home?

No. You must report back to work as soon as is reasonably possible, if you are not required for court. The county registrar can provide a statement of attendance to your employer, if required, and you can be financially penalised by your employer if you do not return to work and are not on jury duty.

Force Majeure Leave

My friends in work talk about force majeure leave. What is it?

Force majeure leave is an entitlement to paid leave for employees "for urgent family reasons, owing to an injury to or the illness of a person specified the immediate presence of the employee at the place where the person is, whether at his or her home or elsewhere, is indispensable" (Parental Leave Act 1998, section 13). The entitlement to this leave is outlined in the Parental Leave Act 1998.

What members of the extended family are covered?

The following relations of the employee are covered under the definition:

- Children (natural and adoptive)
- Spouse, partner (living as husband and wife) or registered civil partner
- Persons for whom the employee acts *in loco parentis*
- Brothers or sisters
- Parents or grandparents

Under the Parental Leave (Amendment) Act 2006, force majeure leave has now been extended to include persons in a relationship of domestic dependency, including same-sex partners.

How much time off can I have?

The maximum time allowable is three days in any predefined consecutive twelve-month period (one year) or five days in any period of thirty-six consecutive months (three years). Any part of a day taken is defined as one full day.

What is the procedure for requesting such leave?

Notice should be given in writing either immediately before or after such leave, clearly specifying the dates requested and a summary of the reason why it is requested.

If disputes arise, an employer may request medical certificates containing the particulars of the injury or illness, and the length of incapacity of the relevant person.

Is force majeure leave counted as continuous employment?
Yes. The employee is deemed to be in full employment during the leave and all employment rights are intact.

My employer has informed me that my old job will not be available when I return from force majeure leave. What are my rights?
If it is not reasonably practicable for the employer to allow an employee return to the position they held prior to the commencement of force majeure leave, the employer must offer the employee suitable alternative employment under a new contract of employment. The new terms must not be substantially less favourable in comparison to their old position.

What if no job exists at all upon my return to work, nor any reasonable prospect of one? What can I do?
An employee who is not entitled to return to work shall be deemed to be dismissed (under the Unfair Dismissals Acts 1977–2001) or to be redundant (Redundancy Payment Acts 1967–2001). In either case the employee may wish to take appropriate action under the Workplace Relations Services.

My childminder is sick. Is this force majeure?
Unfortunately a childminder is not one of the recognised persons covered under the legislation unless they are related to the employee as defined in section 13(2) of the

Parental Leave Act 1998. In addition, a "person of domestic dependency" is defined as a person who resides with an employee and is taken to be in a relationship of domestic dependency with the employee if, in the event of injury or illness, one reasonably relies on the other to make arrangements for the provision of care; the sexual orientation of the person concerned is immaterial, i.e. same or opposite sex (sections 8(*b*)(a) and (b) of the Parental Leave (Amendment) Act 2006). In addition, force majeure leave would also not be applicable if your child's school is closed on a certain day.

Compassionate Leave

My uncle died yesterday. How much paid time off am I entitled to from my employer?
Unfortunately there is no employment legislation in relation to the provision of automatic paid time off for the death of a family member. The allowance of paid time off is purely at the discretion of your employer. Such an agreement is generally included in your terms and conditions of employment or as part of registered collective agreements, Joint Labour Committees (JLCs) or through standard custom and practice within your company.

Is compassionate leave not the same as force majeure leave? Can they be used interchangeably?
No. Force majeure leave is only allowable in urgent or crisis situations in relation to the illness or injury of a family member or relation, where the employee's help is required. Unfortunately, force majeure leave cannot be used after the death of a family member or relative.

SUMMARY CHECKLIST: Force Majeure and Compassionate Leave

Force Majeure Leave

Were you absent from work due to an illness or crisis relating ☐
to a family member?

Did your employer pay you during your absence? ☐

Do you have supporting medical documentation, if required, ☐
to support your application?

Compassionate Leave

What is your employer's policy in relation to compassionate ☐
leave?

What are the terms and conditions in your contract? ☐

Does the leave vary depending on your relationship with the ☐
deceased?

Maternity Leave

How long can I stay in work before my baby is due and how many weeks of leave do I receive?
Since the introduction of the new Maternity Protection (Amendment) Act 2004, employees can work right up to two weeks before the date the child is due and then have twenty-four weeks off after the birth of the child, a total of twenty-six weeks (since 1 March 2007).

Can I take any additional unpaid maternity leave?
Yes, you are eligible (since 1 March 2007) to take an additional sixteen weeks of unpaid maternity leave from your employer. You should inform your employer in writing at least four weeks before your proposed 'return to work' date, requesting additional unpaid maternity leave from your employer if required.

Does my employer have to pay me while I am on maternity leave?

No, your employer does not have to pay you while you are on maternity leave. It is essential to check fully the terms and conditions (contract) of your employment, which may clearly state your employer's policy in relation to payment of maternity leave and eligibility. In some cases, employers pay wages in full during this leave, but in return expect a rebate from the employee under the social welfare Maternity Benefit payment scheme. In Budget 2013 the Minister for Finance announced that Maternity Benefit will be a taxable source of income (previously tax exempt) from 1 July 2013.

What if my employer does not pay me while I'm on maternity leave? Am I still eligible for any payment?

You may be eligible for payment under the social welfare Maternity Benefit payment scheme. There are a number of eligibility criteria for the scheme, and the relevant rate of payment granted to you under the Maternity Benefit scheme is assessed. This payment takes into consideration 80 per cent of your average weekly wage in the 'relevant' tax year, i.e. two years prior to your current claim, up to the maximum rate payable under Maternity Benefit from the Department of Social Protection. Alternatively, you will receive the minimum rate of payment under the scheme if your average weekly wage in the relevant tax year is below the threshold rate defined, subject to your fulfilment of the eligibility criteria, i.e. PRSI contributions.

How soon should I inform my employer I am pregnant?

You should inform your employer as soon as you can confirm you are pregnant. This is essential for your employer to both assess any safety risks associated with your employment or place of employment and, where possible, remove or reduce these risks. It is also advisable to discuss with your employer the proposed commencement date of your maternity leave.

How soon should I apply for my Maternity Benefit payment?

You should apply to the Department of Social Protection at least six weeks before you plan to commence your maternity leave, or twelve weeks if you are self-employed.

Is there any minimum period I must work with my employer to be eligible for maternity leave?

No, there is no minimum period of service required to be completed with your employer before you are eligible for maternity leave, although your employer may set down a minimum period of service completed to be eligible for paid maternity leave from your employer. Alternatively, there are a number of entry requirements to determine if you are eligible for Maternity Benefit payment from the Department of Social Protection.

Is maternity leave counted as continuous employment?

Yes. The employee is deemed to be in full employment during this leave, and all employment rights are protected (including eligibility for public holiday entitlements).

I have worked for my employer for less than twelve months. Can my employer dismiss me for being pregnant?

No. An employee cannot be dismissed for being pregnant, even if they have not completed twelve months of continuous service. There is no minimum requirement for completion of service with reference to dismissal for being pregnant.

Our child was stillborn at week 26. Is my wife entitled to maternity leave?

Yes, women who have stillbirths or miscarriages after the completion of week 24 are entitled to the full maternity leave entitlement of 26 weeks.

My wife had complications after the birth of our child and is now in hospital. Can she postpone her maternity leave?

An employee can, with the consent of her employer, postpone part of her maternity leave (subject to minimum requirements and written notification with supporting documentation) up to a maximum of six months, or re-commence remaining leave within seven days of leaving hospital. This postponement only applies upon hospitalisation of the child and not the mother (Maternity Protection Act 2004).

Am I entitled to paid time off to breastfeed my child? Is my employer under an obligation to provide facilities?

A person who is breastfeeding is entitled, without loss of pay and for 26 weeks following the birth, to either time off work to breastfeed in the workplace or a reduced working day in order to breastfeed at home (up to one hour per day, or by alternative arrangement with your employer). An employer is not required to provide facilities for breastfeeding in the workplace where cost would be more than nominal.

Am I entitled to paid time off for my partner and me to attend antenatal classes?

A pregnant employee is entitled to time off work, without loss of pay, to attend one set of antenatal classes (other than the last three classes). An expectant father is entitled to time off without loss of pay to attend the last two antenatal classes in a set before the birth. Notification of the classes must be provided to the employer no later than two weeks before the expected classes. Late claims (no later than one week) can be accepted by the employer with a valid reason (Maternity Protection Act 2004). Paid time off includes attendance for antenatal care, classes and postnatal care.

What can I do if I am dismissed for being pregnant?
You may take an action under the Unfair Dismissals Acts 1977–2007 (Maternity Protection Act 2004) or under the Employment Equality Acts 1998–2011 (to the Equality Authority (now replaced by the Workplace Relations Services)) under one of the nine grounds of discrimination (i.e. gender, discussed later in the chapter).

I wish to go back to work part-time (from full-time work) after I have my child. Can I do this?
Under new recommendations in addition to the EU Directive on Maternity Leave (Directive 92/85/EEC), new proposals are recommended to provide for an employee to ask for more flexible work arrangements after the end of maternity leave and the employer must give the matter fair consideration, although the employer will have a right to refuse the request. At present there is no compulsion on an employer to accept a request from an employee to change or alter their working hours after maternity leave. Any agreement at present is by mutual consent.

My employer has informed me my old job will not be available when I return. What are my rights?
If it is not reasonably practicable for the employer to allow an employee return to the position they held prior to the commencement of their leave, the employer must offer the employee suitable alternative employment under a new contract of employment. These terms must not be substantially less favourable in comparison to the old position.

What if no job exists at all upon my return to work, nor any reasonable prospect of one? What can I do?
If there is no job for you when you return to work, you shall be deemed to be unfairly dismissed (under the Unfair Dismissals Acts 1977–2007) or to be redundant (Redundancy Payment Acts 1967–2007). In both cases, the employee may wish to take appropriate action through the Workplace Relations Services.

I am on maternity leave at present. Can I be made redundant?
No. An employee on maternity leave cannot be given notice of redundancy until their return to work. Such a date is the proposed return to work date as indicated to the employer. Time on maternity leave can be included for the purpose of calculating redundancy payments.

SUMMARY CHECKLIST: Maternity Leave

Have you informed your employer you are pregnant? What ☐
steps can be taken (regarding the job or environment) to
assist during pregnancy?

Were you dismissed for being pregnant (regardless of the ☐
length of service)?

What is your employer's policy on maternity leave? Does your ☐
employer pay you in full while you're on maternity leave?

Have you complied with the notice periods for unpaid leave? ☐

When you returned to work was your old job available? ☐

Was an alternative position (with similar terms) offered to you ☐
on your return?

Did you avail of accumulated leave due to you whilst on ☐
maternity leave?

Were you made redundant whilst on maternity leave? ☐

Paternity Leave

*My son is due to be born in the next couple of days. What
are my paternity leave entitlements?*
Unfortunately, there is no employment legislation in relation to paternity leave. Therefore any leave granted for the
birth of your son is at the discretion of your employer or
taken from your holiday leave entitlements, if requested.
If you are a civil servant, you may be granted three days
(paid) paternity leave by your employer. Maternity leave
may only be granted to the father for the remaining period
in the event of death of the mother within 24 weeks of the
birth of the child or, if the death occurs more than 24 weeks
after the birth, additional leave may be granted up to week
40 after the death, i.e. maximum 24 weeks and 16 weeks'
unpaid additional leave (Maternity Protection Act 2004).
The leave will start within seven days of the mother's
death. If the father is sick, he may request that this leave be
terminated and that he receives normal sick leave.

What are the paternity rights across Europe?
Ireland is lowest in the league when it comes to paternity rights across Europe. The figures vary from two

days (Spain, Netherlands and Luxembourg), to one week (Portugal), two weeks (UK, Austria, Italy and France), three weeks (Denmark) and four weeks (Finland and Norway), and up to three months' paid time off in Iceland.

A review and possible reform of family entitlements are being considered by the Minister for Justice, Equality and Defence (Parliamentary Questions, 6 June 2012) as part of the proposal in developing the Family Leave Bill (as recommended under Council Directive 2010/18/EU – Framework Agreement on Parent Leave). The proposed Bill may also review more positively existing various family leave legislation (maternity, adoptive, parental and carer's leave) and may provide an opportunity to examine the possibility of additional leave for fathers.

Adoptive Leave

Can I get paid time off work in preparation for an adoption?
The Adoption Leave Act 2005 provides paid time off for parents during working hours to attend preparation classes (pre-adoption meetings). Adoptive leave of sixteen weeks can be taken by an employee (unpaid, unless agreed to be paid by the employer), but only by the adopting mother (exceptions may apply). Such adoptive leave does not affect your employment rights regarding continuity of service or annual leave. Notice should be given to your employer at least four weeks before the proposed commencement of leave. An additional eight weeks of leave may be taken, although the employer must be informed at least four weeks prior to the commencement of the additional leave. Adoptive Benefit may

be available from the Department of Social Protection (subject to eligibility).

Since 30 January 2006, adoptive leave can be split, i.e. the period of sixteen weeks doesn't have to be taken together, and additional adoptive leave may also be granted in the event of the adopted child being hospitalised, subject to agreement from the employer (section 9 of the Act).

SUMMARY CHECKLIST: Paternity and Adoptive Leave

Paternity Leave

Does your employer provide paid paternity leave?	☐
What is your employer's policy on paternity leave?	☐
Adoptive Leave	
Are you adopting a child?	☐
What is your employer's policy on such leave? Is paid leave provided?	☐
Did you comply with the minimum notice for adoptive leave and additional leave?	☐

Parental Leave

I would like to take time off work to be with my children. Can I do this and am I paid for my leave?

Parents (natural, adoptive and persons acting *in loco parentis* in respect of an eligible child), who are employees, may be entitled to fourteen weeks unpaid leave from employment to take care of their children. The purpose of the Act is to promote a more positive family–work balance and to support flexibility in the workplace for employees and employers. EU proposals have extended this period to eighteen weeks across Europe since March 2012 but the Irish Government has sought a twelve-month deferral until 2013 for Irish parents. This will be passed under the proposed Family Leave Bill to implement EU Directive 2010/18/EU on parental leave and to consolidate, with amendments, all family leave legislation.

The new directive will allow the transfer of parental leave entitlement between parents although a minimum of one month cannot be transferrable in full, unless being utilised by the other parent in their own right for the purpose of work–life balance. This has been proposed in an effort to encourage more fathers to take the leave.

My child was born in January 2004 and is now nine. Am I eligible for parental leave?
Firstly, parental leave only applies to children born or adopted after 3 June 1996 and, secondly, parental leave shall end on the date the child is eight years of age (as amended under the Parental Leave (Amendment) Act 2006).

I have only worked for my employer for ten months. Am I eligible for such leave?
Yes, you may be eligible for some pro rata leave, i.e. proportionate leave dependent on the length of service you have completed with your employer. Unfortunately, you must have one year of continuous service with your employer to be eligible for the full fourteen weeks of parental leave, although once you have completed three months of employment you are entitled to one week of leave for each calendar month. Therefore, in your case, you will be eligible for ten weeks of parental leave.

I had twins recently. Am I entitled to 28 weeks of parental leave?
Section 6(7) of the Parental Leave Act 1998 states "here both of the parents of a child are entitled to parental leave

in respect of the child, neither of the parents shall be entitled to the parental leave of the other parent or may transfer any part of the period of his or her parental leave to the other parent", although if both parents work for the same employer then, and only then, can the parental leave be transferred to either parent (as amended in section 3 of the Parental Leave (Amendment) Act 2006. In addition, the law states (section 6(5) of the Parental Leave Act 1998) that "an employee shall be entitled to parental leave in respect of each child of which he or she is the natural or adoptive parent", which therefore implies parental leave entitlement is available for each individual child (including multiple births). This time may be taken together, i.e. consecutively, if approved in advance by the employer.

At present, we are in the process of adopting. The child in question is now seven years old. Is there any possibility we may be eligible for parental leave?
Yes, you may be eligible for parental leave if the child is the subject of an adoption order and has reached the age of three, but has not reached the age of eight prior to the processing of an adoption order. This is subject to a further two years (maximum) after the commencement of the adoption order. The leave must be taken before the child reaches eight years of age, except in certain circumstances in the case of an adopted child. In the case of a child who is under six years at the time of the adoption, the leave must be taken before the child reaches eight years of age. However, if the child is aged between six years and eight years at the time of the adoption, the leave must be taken within two years of the adoption order.

Do I have to take the full fourteen weeks of leave in a continuous period?
No. After consulting with your employer, you may wish to take such leave in any of the following combinations:

- Continuous period of fourteen weeks
- Two blocks of a minimum of six weeks (with a ten-week gap between the two blocks
- A number of weeks of leave spread over a period of time pre-defined between you and the employer
- Days off
- Hours off
- Combination of the above (as agreed with your employer over a pre-defined period of time)

My husband and I both wish to take parental leave. Is this possible? We have two small children; would it be possible for both of us to take parental leave for each?
With reference to both parents, yes, it is possible for you both to apply for parental leave, assuming you meet the requirements set out earlier, i.e. continuous service. With reference to both your young children, it is possible for an individual to take two sets of parental leave, subject to a maximum of fourteen weeks in any pre-defined twelve-month period. Under the Parental Leave (Amendment) Act 2006 parents can transfer parental leave entitlements from one to another if both parents are employed by the same employer, subject to the employer's agreement.

What is the procedure for informing my employer of my request for parental leave?
An employee must inform their employer in writing at least six weeks before the commencement of the proposed

leave. Such notice must be signed and include the proposed duration of the leave and the date of birth of the child. It is requested the employee keep a copy for his or her own records. The employer will then provide the employee with a confirmation document containing all the facts of the agreement.

I was planning to commence my parental leave on 3 December 2012, but my employer gave me a note today (31 November 2012) requesting postponement. Can he do this?
No, your employer may only request postponement at least four weeks before commencement of leave, for a maximum of a further six months, subject to valid grounds, including seasonal variations and operational factors or if another employee is or will be on parental leave at the same time.

However, this postponement will not be possible if both parties have signed a confirmation document.

My employer has informed me my old job will not be available when I return. What are my rights?
If it is not reasonably practicable for the employer to allow an employee to return to the position they held within the company prior to the commencement of their leave, the employer must offer the employee suitable alternative employment under a new contract of employment. Such terms must not be substantially less favourable in comparison to the old position.

What if no job exists at all upon my return to work, nor any reasonable prospect of one? What can I do?
An employee who is prevented from returning to work shall be deemed to be dismissed (under the

Unfair Dismissals Acts 1977–2007) or to be redundant (Redundancy Payment Acts 1967–2007). In both cases, the employee may wish to take appropriate action through the Workplace Relations Services.

I am on parental leave at present. Can I be made redundant?
No. An employee on parental leave cannot be given notice of redundancy until their return to work. Such a date is the proposed return to work date as notified to the employer. Time on parental leave is included for the purpose of calculating redundancy payments.

SUMMARY CHECKLIST: Parental Leave

What age is your child? If your child is aged eight years or under, you may be eligible. ☐

How long have you worked for the company? ☐

Have you adopted? ☐

Have you complied with the minimum notice period? ☐

When you returned to work was your old job available? ☐

Was an alternative position (with similar terms) offered to you on your return? ☐

Were you made redundant whilst on parental leave? ☐

Carer's Leave

I have worked for the last fifteen months with a firm. My mother has a serious medical condition and I would like to take time off work to mind her. Will I lose my job if I do so?
Once an employee has completed at least twelve months of continuous service with the employer, the employee may be eligible for carer's leave. Your position is protected whilst on carer's leave.

I only work part-time (fifteen hours per week) with my employer. Am I also eligible for carer's leave?
There is no minimum hours' threshold for eligibility for carer's leave. Therefore, part-time workers are also eligible.

Who decides if my mother's medical condition is serious or not and how can they decide?
To be eligible for carer's leave, the person for whom you propose to care must need "full-time care and attention". Full-time care and attention is assessed through a medical assessment by the Department of Social Protection.

Do I have to live with my mother and does she have to require 24-hour care for me to be entitled to carer's leave?
Each case will be assessed on its own merits. It is not necessary for 24-hour care and assistance to be required by the cared-for person, and you do not have to live with your mother, although certain factors may be taken into consideration: how far you live from her and how long it would take you to get to her in an emergency; if you have transport or a method of transport in case of an emergency; if you both have telephones or if your mother has a monitoring system in place; and if you have the ability and mobility to fulfil a caring position.

My father also needs full-time care and attention. Do I get carer's leave for my mother and father together or separately?
Generally an employee will not be permitted carer's leave for more than one person. However, you may be eligible to the combined period of 208 weeks (104 weeks for each person being cared for) if both relevant people reside together. In this case, you may be allowed one

continuous combined period of leave for both 'cared-for' persons.

Do I get paid while on carer's leave?

No, you do not get paid directly by your employer while on carer's leave. You may apply for a Carer's Benefit or Carer's Allowance payment from the Department of Social Protection.

In summary, Carer's Benefit is a contribution-based payment assessed on your contributions from employment (PRSI contributions). Carer's Allowance is a means-tested payment taking into consideration whether you are married, in a civil partnership, single or cohabiting, and your financial incomes in relation to your status.

How much time off work can I receive on carer's leave?

You may receive one continuous period of two years (104 weeks), or more than one period (minimum thirteen weeks) up to a total of 104 weeks. An employer may refuse the minimum period of thirteen weeks on reasonable grounds only. Discussions may take place between employer and employee to come to a mutually beneficial agreement.

I am planning to take six months' leave in two parts with four weeks' break in the middle. Is this possible?

No, this is not feasible as the minimum break between intervals must be six weeks. It is also important to consider that the gap between carer's leave for different 'cared-for' persons is six months.

Is my job protected during my carer's leave?

Yes. The time on carer's leave is defined as employment in assessing continuous service and therefore none of your terms and conditions of employment will be affected during such leave.

How are my annual leave and public holiday entitlements affected by my carer's leave?

After the first thirteen weeks on carer's leave, no annual leave entitlement is gained. Therefore, if a public holiday falls during your first thirteen-week period of carer's leave, you may be eligible (pro rata) to the public holiday entitlement (see sections on public holidays and holiday entitlements), but if the public holiday falls after your first thirteen weeks of carer's leave, you are not entitled to the public holiday entitlement. The first thirteen weeks' leave is counted as continuous service in the calculation of annual leave.

I am planning to take carer's leave. What is the procedure with my employer?

You must give your employer at least six weeks' notice in writing of your request for carer's leave. Such written notice must include:

- Date of commencement
- Duration of proposed leave and proposed intervals
- Application and approval of request from the Department of Social Protection
- Employee's signature and dated application

I need to commence my carer's leave immediately, due to my mother's illness. Is this possible?

In such cases, it is essential to inform your employer as soon as is reasonably practicable. Your employer may use their discretion to approve or reject such application. If immediate leave is disallowed, your employer must state reasonable grounds for their decision and the employee may appeal.

How do I know from my employer whether or not I have been approved for such leave?

Upon receipt of approval from the Department of Social Protection, your employer must furnish you with a confirmation document at least two weeks before your commencement date, which must clearly state the date of commencement of leave and the duration of leave, and include the signature of both parties (employer and employee).

I am planning to return to work after being on carer's leave. What is the procedure regarding notice and what is my position regarding returning to my old job?

An employee should inform their employer not less than four weeks before the proposed return date. Although not compulsory, it would be advisable to provide notice in writing for clarification purposes. An employee is entitled to return to work for their employer in the job held prior to the leave and under the same terms and conditions of employment.

My employer has informed me my old job will not be available when I return. What are my rights?

If it is not reasonably practicable for the employer to allow an employee to return to work in their old position, the employer must offer the employee suitable alternative employment under a new contract of employment. Such terms must not be substantially less favourable in comparison to their old position.

What if no job exists at all upon my return to work, nor any reasonable prospect of one? What can I do?

An employee who is not entitled to return to work shall be deemed to be dismissed (under the Unfair Dismissals Acts 1977–2007) or to be redundant (Redundancy Payment Acts 1967–2007). In both cases the employee may wish to take appropriate action through the Workplace Relations Services.

SUMMARY CHECKLIST: Carer's Leave

How long have you worked for your employer?	☐
Has the 'cared-for' person been assessed for "full-time care and attention"?	☐
Are you eligible for Carer's Benefit/Allowance or carer's leave?	☐
Have you agreed with your employer how the leave can be taken?	☐
Have you received confirmation from your employer?	☐
Have you assessed any leave due during your first thirteen weeks of carer's leave?	☐
When returning to work, have you complied with the minimum notice?	☐
When you returned to work was your old job available?	☐
Was an alternative position (with similar terms) offered to you on your return?	☐
Were you made redundant whilst on carer's leave?	☐

Protection of Part-Time Workers

I am a part-time worker. What are my rights compared to my full-time colleagues?

The Protection of Employees (Part-Time Work) Act 2001 came into operation to provide that a part-time employee cannot be treated in a less favourable manner than a comparable full-time employee in relation to conditions of employment. The Act also ensures that all employee legislation currently applying to full-time employees is also fully available to part-time employees (subject to certain criteria).

Who is a 'comparable' employee?

A comparable employee is a full-time employee (of the same or opposite sex) with whom a part-time employee compares themselves. The following conditions must apply:

- The comparable employee and part-time employee are employed by the same or an associated employer.
- The part-time employee (if the sole employee) has a relevant full-time employee identified in a collective agreement (i.e. defined in a relevant sector and identified by the Department of Jobs, Enterprise and Innovation).
- The full-time employee is employed in the same industry or sector of employment as the part-time employee.

In comparing employees, it is important to consider whether:

- Both employees perform the same work under the same or similar conditions, or each is interchangeable with the other in relation to work, and differences are of small importance or occur with such irregularity as to be seen as insignificant.
- The work performed by the part-time employee is equal or greater in value to the work performed by the other employee concerned (considering skill, physical

and mental requirements, responsibility and working conditions).

My friend is an agency worker. Who is her relevant comparable employee?

The Act states that agency workers can only compare themselves to a comparable employee who is also an agency worker. This implies part-time workers cannot compare themselves to agency workers. This did not change with the passing of the Protection of Employees (Temporary Agency Work) Act 2012 in May 2012 as stated in section 9 of that Act.

If I am a comparable employee (part-time), what benefits will I really gain?

Essentially, your employment benefits are comparable to those of a full-time employee. Such benefits include overtime rates, and holiday and public holiday entitlements.

Protection of Fixed-Term Workers

I have heard about the Protection of Fixed-Term Workers Act. What is it?

The Protection of Employees (Fixed-Term Work) Act 2003, commonly known as the Protection of Fixed-Term Workers Act, was implemented to remove discrimination against fixed-term workers when compared to permanent employees, as well as providing a structure of fairness in comparison to permanent ('comparable') employees. Essentially, the Act ensures a fixed-term employee will not be treated less favourably than a permanent employee in relation to overtime, holiday entitlements (subject to minimum entitlements) and pensions.

What is a fixed-term contract?

A fixed-term contract includes a fixed time (specific period), completion of a specific task (certain project) or completion of a specific event (e.g. launch of website).

I am a trainee nurse. Am I covered under the Act?

No. The following categories are not covered under the Act:

- Agency workers placed by a temporary work agency at the disposal of a contractor employer
- Apprentices
- Members of the Defence Forces
- Trainee Gardaí
- Trainee nurses
- Those in publicly supported training or vocational re-training

However, employees working under a contract of employment as any of the following are covered under the Act:

- Qualified Gardaí
- Civil servants
- HSE members
- Vocational Education Committee staff

Who is a 'comparable' employee in relation to the Act?

A comparable employee (section 5), in relation to permanent and fixed-term workers, is one who:

- Performs the same work as the other
- Has the same or similar conditions
- Has a position that is interchangeable with that of the other

- Performs work that is the same or of a similar nature to that of the other
- Performs work, including skill, responsibility and conditions, that is of equal or greater value (regardless whether the person is permanent or on a fixed-term contract) or
- If a sole employee, the permanent employee is a comparable employee in a defined sector of employment or as part of a collective agreement

An employer can refrain from making you permanent, and continue to treat you less favourably, if he or she has valid grounds. Section 7 of the Protection of Employees (Fixed-Term Work) Act 2003 clearly states that an employer can refuse to make an employer permanent if it is "for the purpose of achieving a legitimate objective of the employer and such treatment is appropriate and necessary for that purpose". Each case will have to be assessed upon its own merits to see if it is a justifiable decision by the employer or not subject to the factors.

My contract is coming to an end next week. What should I expect my employer to do?
Your employer must provide you in writing, on or before the end of your fixed-term contract (section 8), with an objective reason why your fixed-term contract may not be renewed and the reason why such contract should not be permanent (i.e. of indefinite duration).

I have completed two years on a fixed-term contract. When can I be made permanent?
An employer must not have an employee on a continuous fixed-term contract for more than four years (section 9).

After three years of continuous employment, an employer may renew such a contract for a further fixed term of one year only.

My employer offered a permanent position to my colleague without notifying the other fixed-term workers. Can she do this?
No. Your employer must make all employees (including fixed-term) aware of all opportunities in the company (section 10). This may be done through putting up a general notice in a suitable place. Similarly, access to training must be, as far as practicable, alike for all employees. In addition, employees must not be penalised or treated differently for trying to enforce their rights under this Act (section 13).

SUMMARY CHECKLIST: Protection of Part-Time and Fixed-Term Workers

Part-Time Employees

Are you treated in a similar way to a full-time employee? ☐

Who is your comparable employee? ☐

Are you an agency worker? ☐

Protection of Fixed-Term Employees

Are you treated in a similar way to a full-time employee? ☐

Are you eligible under the Act? ☐

Who is your comparable employee? ☐

How long are you on a fixed-term contract? ☐

Have you been informed of the reason why your contract was not renewed? ☐

Do you have the same access to training or new positions? ☐

Employer–Employee Disputes

My employer is planning to move premises shortly. This will cause inconvenience regarding my travel arrangements, and incur extra costs for me. What are my rights in relation to 'disturbance money'?

'Disturbance money' (payment for the inconvenience) is a discretionary payment paid by your employer. There is no automatic entitlement to such payment. Therefore it would be advisable to liaise with your employer (or representative body) to try to negotiate such a situation. Factors that may be taken into account include:

- The proposed distance (radius) from the existing premises to the proposed new premises. There has been a precedent dependent on the distance of the new location compared to the existing location. As an indicator (but not definitive) a distance (radius) of 20 miles (32 km) could be considered as a fundamental change in the terms and conditions of employment.
- The proposed inconvenience caused (time and cost) by the move
- The notice period given of such change
- Proposed alternative changes in working arrangements
- Is such a change fundamental in nature to your contract?
- Is there a possibility you can seek redundancy/ constructive dismissal?

Therefore, in summary, any agreements between you and your employer would tend to be by negotiation or by the possible intervention of the Labour Court.

I have a dispute with my employer. What should I do?
Firstly, it would be advisable to try to resolve the issue with your employer in an informal manner. It is essential, therefore, to inform your employer clearly of any breach or dispute, clearly stating the issues and proposed outcomes.

If such an approach is not achievable or viable, it may be advisable to implement the company's grievance procedure with your employer. The grievance procedure should be available within your terms and conditions of employment or employee handbook. This procedure should set down the steps and time frames for resolution. If there is no grievance procedure in place, or in the terms and conditions of your employment, a Code of Practice (Grievance and Disciplinary Procedures – August 2006, incorporated by SI 146/2000, Industrial Relations Act 2000) provides some general guidelines in this area and should be the recommended model if there are no alternative procedures in place. The Code is available from www.workplacerelations.ie.

Alternatively, if you are a member of a union, you should contact your union representative to discuss your problem. Structures may be in place at local levels to discuss or resolve any issues.

The Employees (Provision of Information and Consultation) Act 2006 will now assist industrial relations between employer and employee in the workplace. The purpose of the Act, which implements EU Directive 2002/14/EC of 11 March 2002, is to provide for the establishment of a general framework setting out minimum requirements for the employee's right to information and consultation in undertakings with at least 50 employees.

It provides a general right to information and consultation for employees from their employer on matters which directly affect them. Alternatively, workplace mediation is available from the Workplace Relations Services, where parties may wish to resolve the matter without taking legal action. Mediation may be advisable where there is a breakdown in the working relationship between the parties. Mediation is voluntary, confidential and impartial. Applications (where both parties are willing to participate) can be made to mediation@lrc.ie. Further details are available on www.workplacerelations.ie.

Alternatively, conciliation may be an alternative option. Conciliation is an extension of direct negotiations, with an independent chairperson to explore possible avenues of settlement. Again, this is a voluntary process with agreement by consensus.

The Protected Disclosure in the Public Interest Bill proposes to provide protection against reprisals and victimisation and redress for workers who disclose information regarding serious wrongdoing in the workplace. The Whistleblowers Protection Bill 2010 was absorbed into section 20 of the Criminal Justice Act 2011 which provides protection against injury, damage, loss or penalisation by an employer for employees who make certain disclosures "reasonably and in good faith" in relation to the conduct of the business and affairs of their employers to the Gardaí. Section 20 of the Criminal Justice Act 2011 states "an employer shall not penalise or threaten penalisation against an employee, or cause or permit any other person to penalise or threaten penalisation against an employee for making a disclosure or for giving evidence in relation to such disclosure in any proceedings relating to a relevant offence" and reporting the matter to the Gardaí. The

offences reported can be in relation to banking, investment and financial activities, breaches of company law,
money laundering, terrorism, theft, fraud, taking part in
a pyramid scheme or destroying data. In addition, the
Protected Disclosure in the Public Interest Bill proposes to
protect whistleblowers who speak out against wrongdoing or cover-ups, whether in the public or private sector,
and protect employees from civil and criminal liability.

What if my issue or dispute cannot be resolved locally?
At present (December 2012), reform has commenced on
improving and simplifying the complaints process. This
reform will be fully implemented with the passing of
the proposed Workplace Relations (Law Reform) Bill.
The Bill will provide for the establishment of a statutory Workplace Relations Commission (WRC) with a full
range of functions previously carried out by the National
Employment Rights Authority (NERA), the Equality
Tribunal, the Labour Relations Commission (LRC),
which includes the Rights Commissioner Service, and the
Employment Appeals Tribunal (EAT) for first-line complaints. The Bill will also provide for the Labour Court
to be the only appeal body to determine appeals against
decisions of WRC adjudicators. In addition, the Bill will
provide for the orderly winding down of NERA, the
Equality Tribunal, the EAT and the LRC, and the transfer
of redundancy appeals to social welfare appeals officers.

Since January 2012, a new single complaint form has
been implemented to replace the previous 30 separate application forms, which would have covered over
110 different complaint types. For all new complaints,
information must be submitted on this new form (available from www.workplacerelations.ie). At present, each

complaint can be selected from a number of 'drop-down' options and therefore one form can cover multiple complaints. As of December 2012, the complaint information must be submitted on the online form and when complete the form must be printed and signed by the person making the complaint. All completed and signed complaint forms since January 2012 are administered by Workplace Relations Customer Service, Department of Jobs, Enterprise and Innovation, O'Brien Road, Carlow. It is proposed that later in 2012 a fully end-to-end online application process will be available.

At present, completed forms received may be considered under the Early Resolution Service. This involves an initial assessment and contact with the parties to the dispute to see if they would be willing (voluntarily) to take part in an early resolution process where the parties could seek to resolve this issue through tri-party contact or communications that is acceptable to all parties. If this cannot be resolved, this does not affect your option, or time frame, to proceed through the normal adjudication process.

Until the passing of the new Bill, completed forms are processed to the existing relevant forum, i.e. the Rights Commissioner Service, Equality Tribunal, Employment Appeals Tribunal, National Employment Rights Authority Inspection Service or Labour Court.

The Rights Commissioner Service is a less formal procedure. It is essential to complete your application correctly, including the correct official company name (either on your payslip or as registered with the Companies Registration Office (www.cro.ie)) and all correct details, and to submit your claim on time. Late applications may be 'out of time' and are therefore not applicable. Upon receipt, a copy of the application is forwarded to the employer by the WRC within five days of the complaint being lodged. An employer may appeal the application (at present and only until the passing of the new Bill), which then must be submitted to the EAT (unfair dismissal cases only). When the Bill is passed all applications will be dealt with through the Workplace Relations Services and may either be resolved through the early resolution process or be referred for hearing to the WRC, which will replace the existing Rights Commissioner Service. This means that the EAT will then be replaced completely for all new cases and will remain in place until the completion of all existing cases.

If the application is not appealed, a date of hearing is set for both parties to meet to discuss the issue and the Rights Commissioner will investigate the complaint and set down recommendations.

At present we have seen a vast reduction in waiting times for Rights Commissioner hearing time frames (from on average six months down to approximately two to three months from date of receipt), although some Employment Appeals Tribunal hearings were delayed for up to a maximum of two years. Under the Workplace Relations (Law Reform) Bill the maximum waiting period for a hearing of first instance will be three months from the date the complaint is lodged.

Will such a complaint affect my standing with my employer?
A complaint should not affect your standing with your employer and should not be used against you at any time in the future. If it is, you may have future grounds for complaint under victimisation laws.

Do I need a solicitor to represent me?

No, you are not required to have legal representation in such cases, although you may wish to do so. Representation at such hearings may be provided solely by you, by your union representative or, alternatively, by an advocate.

Is the hearing a public hearing? Can anyone attend and will it be recorded in the newspaper?

No. All Rights Commissioner hearings are held in private and are only attended by the relevant parties, i.e. employer, employee (and representative if required) and Rights Commissioner (a minor exception can apply under the Payment of Wages Act 1991). All recommendations are private and are not in the public domain.

This is proposed to be changed under the new Workplace Relations (Law Reform) Bill, where all cases will be reported and will be available on www.workplac-erelations.ie. Either party to the adjudication may request anonymity in the published decision. Such a request, which must be accompanied by the reason why anonymity is sought, will be considered by the Workplace Relations Commission adjudicator, who will decide whether or not the request will be granted. Where anonymity is granted the decision will be published with the names and any identifying features concerned removed.

What do I have to do at such hearings?

Generally, a written submission will have to be presented prior to or on the day in question, clearly stating the issue of complaint, the background, the areas of dispute and the proposed outcome by either party. Both sides will present their own relevant submissions and such submissions will be cross-examined by the Rights Commissioner to clarify all points for investigation.

Will the Rights Commissioner make a decision at the hearing?
In some cases, the Rights Commissioner may propose recommendations between parties where feasible on the day in question. Alternatively, the Commissioner may take some time to reflect upon submissions and forward written recommendations within an appropriate time frame.

To date (December 2012), all applications are centrally administered by the Workplace Relations Services for all complaints through the completion of one single complaint form, and upon receipt are then distributed under the existing frameworks, i.e. Rights Commissioner Service, EAT, Equality Tribunal, National Employment Rights Inspectorate Service and the Labour Court. All of these bodies currently administer their complaints separately and the formalities, requirements, assessments, time frames and interventions vary with each body. The proposed changes to be implemented under the Workplace Relations (Law Reform) Bill will set down a common standard for dispute resolution for WRC hearings (which will replace all the existing hearing bodies). In addition, all hearings must comply with the principles of natural justice. Therefore, while hearings of the WRC will not follow strict rules similar to courts of law, fair procedures should be followed.

The legislation will make provision for the Minister for Jobs, Enterprise and Innovation to make regulations to provide for certain matters in relation to the conduct of hearings. Hearings of the Workplace Relations Commission will be held in private unless the WRC adjudicator decides at the request of either party to the complaint to hear the complaint in public. Parties wishing their case to be heard in public will be required to submit their request for a hearing in public and the reasons in writing in advance of the hearing. All parties will be consulted in advance as to the decision.

All decisions will comply with a common template clearly detailing the reason, facts and relevant legislation. In addition, it is proposed that 90 per cent of all decisions will be provided with 28 working days of the hearing, and will be available online at www.workplacerelations. ie within ten working days.

How much does the service cost?
The service is free, unless the Commissioner sees such a case to be frivolous. However, if you have legal representation such costs will have to be paid by you, the employee. Legal costs are not granted to either party in the case of awards.

Under the new Workplace Relations (Law Reform) Bill the possibility of imposing administrative fees for paper-based applications and possibly for appeal applications is being considered, but there has been no confirmation to date (December 2012).

If I am not happy with the Rights Commissioner's recommendations, what can I do?
An appeal must be lodged within six weeks of the receipt of the recommendation. This appeal will be forwarded to the EAT. In some situations, cases may be referred upon appeal to the Labour Court.

Under the new Workplace Relations (Law Reform) Bill a standard consistent time limit of 42 days from the date of the decision will be imposed and will be implemented by a single appeal body only, i.e. the Labour Court, for all appeals. The written decision from the WRC hearing will provide the basis for any appeal. A party who fails to attend (or be represented at) a WRC hearing, without reasonable cause, shall lose the right to appeal to the Labour Court. Appeals will be heard in public and all appeals will be published on www.workplacerelations.ie. The Labour Court will act as a court of final appeal for all adjudication decisions of the Workplace Relations Commission, subject to the right of either party to bring a further appeal from a determination of the Labour Court to the High Court on a point of law only.

What if I have been granted an award but my employer does not carry out the recommendation?
If the recommendation is not appealed within the time frame (six weeks) and the awards have not been enforced within the specified time period, the employee may then forward a complaint to the EAT for implementation (once the EAT is wound down complaints should be made to the Labour Court). Such implementation orders are similar in nature to orders made by judges in the Circuit Court. In some other cases (dependent on the legislation the case is under), non-implementation may be referred to the Circuit Court. Interest may be awarded for the six-week period. In such cases, the superior body simply reinforces the award and does not hear any new evidence in relation to the case.

There is no clarity as yet (December 2012) under the new Workplace Relations (Law Reform) Bill as to what is the most effective method of enforcing awards but it is agreed a centralised new system should be devised for all legislation.

Why should I choose the process of the Rights Commissioner service over the EAT?

The Rights Commissioner service is less formal – a private hearing – and to some may be seen as less daunting. The issue can generally be resolved more promptly, does not require witnesses to attend and cases can be represented by you, the employee. The EAT is more formal in structure (three-person panel), is a public hearing (anyone can attend), is publicly reported and witnesses may be called to attend (costs of witnesses may be charged to the relevant party). In most cases, employees may appoint legal representation (although this is not compulsory). Alternatively, some cases may be taken through the Equality Tribunal (covering breaches of the Employment Equality Act 2008 and victimisation).

Under the new Workplace Relations (Law Reform) Bill, the Rights Commissioner and Employment Appeals Tribunal (EAT) will be merged into part of the new, first-instance Workplace Relations Commission.

Who is the three-person (EAT) panel made up of?

The panel consists of a chairperson (solicitor or barrister of not less than seven years' standing) and representation from both an employer's body (e.g. Irish Businesses and Employers Confederation (IBEC)) and an employee's body (e.g. Irish Congress of Trade Unions (ICTU)).

Does compensation vary depending on the method of recourse?

No, generally awards from the Rights Commissioner or the EAT do not vary. In most cases such awards are dependent on the relevant breach, compensatory awards due to such breach, outstanding payments due to the employee and relevant contributory negligence (percentage fault by either side) of either party.

The maximum award in unfair dismissal cases is 104 weeks (two years') service.

At present, claims that arise on the termination of the employment relationship, in general, can be made directly to the EAT and include claims for unfair dismissal under the Unfair Dismissal Acts, claims for redundancy payment under the Redundancy Payments Act, claims for minimum notice entitlements under the Minimum Notice and Terms of Employment Acts and claims for holiday entitlements under the Organisation of Working Time Act. Claims for unfair dismissal can be made in the first instance to the Rights Commissioner, but can be objected to by the employee/employer and, if so, can be referred to the EAT.

Claims that arise during the continuation of the employment relationship in general are made to the Rights Commissioner Service. Certain Rights Commissioner case recommendations (under certain legislation) can be appealed (at present) to the Labour Court.

ACT	RC* (1st Instance)	EAT (1st Instance)	EAT (Appeal)
Unfair Dismissals Act	√	√	√
Payment of Wages Act	√		√
Terms of Employment (Information) Act	√		√
Maternity Protection Act	√		√
Adoptive Leave Act	√		√
Protection of Young Persons Act	√		√

(Continued)

(Continued)			
ACT	RC* (1st Instance)	EAT (1st Instance)	EAT (Appeal)
Protection of Persons Reporting Child Abuse Act	√		√
National Minimum Wage Act	√		√
Protection of Employees (Part-Time and Fixed-Time) Act	√		√
Organisation of Working Time Act	√	√	√
Parental Leave Act	√		√
Carer's Leave Act	√		√
Protection of Employees (Employers' Insolvency) Acts		√	
Redundancy Payment Act		√	
Minimum Notice and Terms of Employment Act	√	√	
Protection of Employees on Transfer of Undertakings	√		√

*Rights Commissioner

Upon the passing of the new Workplace Relations (Law Reform) Bill, all complaints will either be resolved through the Early Resolution Service or referred for hearing (in the first instance) to the Workplace Relations Commission only. Any cases appealed thereafter can only be appealed to the Labour Court.

It is important to note that since January 2012, under the new single Workplace Relations Complaint Form, you do not have to know to which body you have to submit your complaint to, as your application will be assessed upon receipt. In addition, the most important factor in making your complaint is to ensure you capture all complaints separately on the form, and ensure you record all the correct employer details.

Under the new Workplace Relations (Law Reform) Bill all complaints, in the first instance, will be considered by the Workplace Relations Commission.

So what cases can I take to the Rights Commissioner and the EAT at present (until the passing of the new Bill)?
The above table explains:

- Cases that can be taken (under the relevant Acts) in the first instance with the Rights Commissioner and the EAT
- Cases that can be taken on appeal from the Rights Commissioner to the EAT

Upon the passing of the new Workplace Relations (Law Reform) Bill, all complaints will either be resolved through the Early Resolution Service or referred for hearing (in the first instance) to the Workplace Relations Commission only. Any cases appealed thereafter can only be appealed to the Labour Court.

So, what are the time frames for making complaints to either the employer, the Rights Commissioner or the EAT?
The following table explains the time frames within which complaints should be made to the relevant body, depending on the type of complaint and the employee's eligibility.

Act	Eligibility	Complaining Body	Time Frames for Complaints
Unfair Dismissals Act 1977–2005	1 year of service	Rights Commissioner EAT	Within 6 months of dismissal (12 months in exceptional circumstances)
Payment of Wages Act 1991	As applicable	Rights Commissioner EAT	6 months from date of deduction (12 months in exceptional circumstances)
Terms of Employment (Information) Act 1994	2 months after commencement, within 2 months of request	Rights Commissioner EAT	6 months after ceasing employment or during employment
Maternity Protection Acts 1994–2004	No minimum time frame	Rights Commissioner EAT Equality Authority	Within 6 months of date of contravention (12 months in exceptional circumstances)
Protection of Young Persons Act 1996	No minimum time frame	Rights Commissioner EAT	Within 6 months of breach (12 months in exceptional circumstances)

(Continued)

(Continued)

Act	Eligibility	Complaining Body	Time Frames for Complaints
National Minimum Wage Act 2000	Employer responds within 4 weeks of request	Rights Commissioner	Within 6 months of date of contravention (12 months if the Rights Commissioner allows)
National Minimum Wage Act 2000 (unfair dismissal)	No minimum time frame	Rights Commissioner	Within 6 months of dismissal (12 months in exceptional circumstances)
Protection of Employees (Part-Time) Act 2001	As applicable	Rights Commissioner	Within 6 months of date of contravention (12 months due to reasonable cause)
Protection of Employees (Part-Time) Act 2001 (unfair dismissal)	No minimum time frame	Rights Commissioner	Within 6 months of dismissal (12 months in exceptional circumstances)
Protection of Employees (Fixed-Time) Act 2003	No minimum time frame	Rights Commissioner	Within 6 months of breach (12 months due to reasonable cause)
Organisation of Working Time Act 1997	No minimum time frame	Rights Commissioner	Within 6 months of date of contravention (12 months due to reasonable cause)

(Continued)

(Continued)

Act	Eligibility	Complaining Body	Time Frames for Complaints
Carer's Leave Act 2001 (entitlement)	1 year of service **not required**	Rights Commissioner	Within 12 months of occurrence of dispute (12 months in exceptional circumstances)
Carer's Leave Act 2001 (unfair dismissal)	1 year of service **not required**	Rights Commissioner	Within 6 months of dismissal (12 months in exceptional circumstances)
Redundancy Payment Acts 1967–2007	2 years of service	EAT	Within 1 year of redundancy (may be extended to 2 years)
Minimum Notice and Terms of Employment Act 1973	After 13 weeks	EAT	Within 6 months of dismissal (may be extended to 2 years)
Protection of Employees on Transfer of Undertakings Regulations 2003	No minimum requirement	Rights Commissioner	Within 6 months of contravention (12 months in exceptional circumstances)

Upon the passing of the new Workplace Relations (Law Reform) Bill all complaints will either be resolved through the Early Resolution Service or referred for hearing (in the first instance) to the Workplace Relations Commission only. Any cases appealed thereafter can only be appealed to the Labour Court.

Under the new Workplace Relations (Law Reform) Bill all complaints regardless must be submitted to the Workplace Relations Services within six months; this may be extended to twelve months in exceptional circumstances. In addition, the Registration Service, which is part of the Workplace Relations Services, will check all complaints on receipt and reject or redirect incomplete complaints, complaints which are out of time or those which are incorrectly grounded. This decision may be appealed to the Labour Court by providing a written submission. If approved, the complaint can then be heard or assessed under the Early Resolution Service or Workplace Commissioner Service.

Are there any other proposed changes in the Workplace Relations (Law Reform) Bill?
Yes, in addition, the proposed legislation will provide assistance through the provision of additional codes of practices to assist employer–employee relationships as well as assist in providing clear and unambiguous information to both employers and employees to assist in resolving work disputes as well as providing a letter template to assist employees inform their employers of issues before seeking redress through the WRC.

In addition, inspectors (under the NERA Inspectorate Service) will become compliance officers to ensure inspection and enforcement of rights after carrying out inspections. Increased powers will be granted to impose on-the-spot fines of in the region of €150 to be paid within fourteen days. Unpaid fines could then be implemented or appealed through the District Court. Compliance officers will also support a voluntary code of compliance with employers. Investigative reports may also be considered as evidence from compliance officers in WRC hearings.

CHAPTER 3

Family and Children

Guardianship

What is guardianship and what relevance does it have?
Guardianship is having an input in relation to major decisions in the upbringing and parenting of the child. This may include decisions in relation to religious and educational upbringing.

Does guardianship have any major impact in relation to caring for the child on a day-to-day basis?
Yes. A specific example would be if the child had an accident and was brought to hospital. A guardian has the right to give consent for the child to undergo any operation. Therefore, in the absence of guardianship, a biological parent or parent acting *in loco parentis*, i.e. as if they were a parent, either of the opposite or same sex, who is not granted guardianship may not have the right to give consent in such a situation. This may delay such decision making in a critical situation.

Also, guardianship may assist in achieving or restoring custody of the child.

I am an unmarried father and my name is on the birth certificate. Am I an automatic guardian of the child?

No. The name on the birth certificate for an unmarried father does not confer any automatic rights. In non-married relationships, the mother is the automatic guardian of the child.

The father may apply for guardianship with the consent of the mother (Children Act 1997, section 4) through the completion of a statutory declaration (form) (SI 5/1998). If an agreement is made, it is essential for the father to mind this form carefully, as no central registration of guardianship forms exists. This is important in any future dispute between parties.

Alternatively, guardianship can be sought through the District Courts (Status of Children Act 1987, section 12) if a formal agreement cannot be made between parties.

My partner has just had a child; we are unmarried. What is the procedure in picking a surname and do I have to put my name on the birth certificate?

Firstly, in registering the birth, you may add your details (as father) to the birth certificate. This will give you the option to choose a surname, which may be:

- Mother's surname
- Father's surname (if father's details are on the birth certificate)
- Double-barrelled surname

Can my name as father be put on the birth certificate without my consent?
In most cases no, this is not feasible, as the father must sign a specialised form (SI 5/1998 – Guardianship of Children (Statutory Declaration) Regulations 1998) confirming he is the father of the child, which allows his details to be registered on the birth certificate.

In other cases, although the father's name is not on the birth certificate, details can be added if a copy of a court order states the person is the father (on grounds of maintenance or access).

I had a child with my partner. At that time we registered my details only. Can I now add my partner's details and change the child's surname?
This can be possible. In such cases, a re-registration can take place adding the father's details and re-registering a surname if required (cases prior to October 1997).

If registration took place after October 1997 and you require re-registration (adding the father's details), the change in surname can only take place with the consent of both parents.

My partner and I had a child together three years ago. At that time we were in a stable relationship and registered the child's surname as that of the father. Since then we have split up and I would like to change my child's surname. Is this possible?
It may not be possible to re-register, as both names were on the birth certificate. In this situation the original document cannot be changed.

The only options available are to change the child's name by deed poll (in the Four Courts) or by common usage. Common usage occurs when an alternative surname is used on a day-to-day basis. Documentary proof may be required when an alternative name is commonly used, e.g. documents used by doctors, schools, dentists, etc.

As a non-married father I am worried about the guardianship of my child if I die. Can I take any steps now to appoint someone in the case of my death?
Yes, steps may be taken to appoint what is known as a testamentary guardian (Guardianship of Infants Act 1964, section 7). This can be carried out by will or specific deed. Such a testamentary guardian is appointed to act with the surviving parent in the best interests of the child.

What if the surviving parent objects to these arrangements?
If the surviving parent objects to the testamentary guardian, they may take the case to court. The court, upon consideration, may assess the application and enforce joint guardianship between the surviving parent and the testamentary guardian. The court has the power to remove guardianship from a parent and appoint it to the testamentary guardian if the best interests of the child are not being considered, i.e. the existing guardian is deemed to be unfit (Guardianship of Infants Act 1964, sections 7(6) and 8). Therefore, all factors in relation to the case must be assessed on a case-by-case basis.

We are planning to marry shortly and have a child together. Will my status as the father in relation to guardianship change after marriage?

Yes, your status may change after marriage, as guardianship is automatically granted if both parents are married at the time of birth or married at some time after the birth of the child.

I am a married father. What rights do I have in relation to guardianship?
Married couples have automatic guardianship upon the birth of their child (Guardianship of Infants Act 1964, section 6(1)). Therefore, it would be presumed that the husband and wife are actually the biological parents of any children born within their marriage.

What if the father of my child is not my husband and I wish to register the biological father's name on the birth certificate?
In such cases the (biological) father must sign a statement stating he is the father of the child. Also, you must also have one of the following:

- A sworn statement from your husband stating he is not the father
- A deed of separation and a statement saying you were separated from your husband for more than ten months before the birth of the child
- A divorce at least ten months before the child was born
- A court order naming the biological father as father, i.e. maintenance, access, etc.

My former partner had a child. She tells me I am the father. I am not sure. What can I do?
If the question of paternity is in dispute, it is possible to have a paternity test done. Such tests are available

nationwide. If the results are positive, the father's details still cannot be added to the birth certificate at that stage unless either agreed to by the mother (and then the initial registration of birth takes place with both parents) via a signed declaration by both parents or, alternatively, the details can be added to the birth certificate (upon re-registration of the birth certificate by both parents adding the father's details). Alternatively, if the mother still disagrees or declines to consent to adding the father's details to the birth certificate he can request a court order confirming paternity which can allow him be registered as the biological father on the birth certificate.

Can the court decide if I am the father or not without proof from a paternity test?

Yes, it may be possible for a court to decide that a person is a parent of the child, but only on proof of the "balance of probabilities" on the facts presented (Status of Children Act 1987, section 15).

Have there been any proposals to make changes to provide automatic rights to fathers?

In 2010 the Law Reform Commission published a recommendation on the legal aspect of family relationships on the family rights and responsibilities of fathers and grandparents. The consultation paper proposed automatic guardianship rights for fathers regardless of marital status, unless it is not in the child's best interests. The consultation paper also examined changing the terminology – from "guardianship", "custody" and "access" to "parental responsibility", "day-to-day care" and "contact" – as well as considering a greater input for stepparents and grandparents. The Commission recommended that automatic parental responsibility be linked to compulsory joint registration upon the birth of a child. The Civil Registration (Amendment) (No. 2) Bill proposes to provide for further amendments to the Civil Registration Act 2004 in relation to the registration of births and deaths, to validate embassy marriages/civil partnerships, to prevent marriages of convenience and to make a number of other amendments. Publication of the Bill is expected in 2013.

Adoption

I am planning to marry my existing partner. I have a child from a previous relationship. Will my husband have any legal rights in relation to my child?
No, not directly. If your husband wishes to have a legal relationship with your child, both parents (including you) must adopt the child. In such cases the biological father must be consulted and, if he is a guardian of the child, his consent is required. Alternatively, you may appoint your husband a testamentary guardian in your will, if required.

Under the Adoption Act 2010, a child may be adopted by married couples (section 33(1)(*a*)(i)), or may be adopted by their mother, father or a relative (section 33 (1)(*a*)(ii)). The Act defines a "parent" as being the mother or father or both of the child, whether or not they are married to each other.

Under the legislation, it is possible for a single person to adopt only if the Adoption Authority considers it in the best interests of the child. This means that if you are living with a same-sex or opposite-sex partner you may apply to the Authority to adopt a child in your own right, even if you plan to raise the child with your partner. However, your partner would have no legal rights in relation to the child. Rights to civil partners, under the Civil Partnership and Certain Rights and Obligations of Cohabitants Act 2010, do not provide civil partners with the same rights of adoption as married couples.

What if the father of the child cannot be contacted? Can the adoption go ahead?

The Adoption Board must complete all reasonable steps to seek consultation with the father before approving the adoption. In some situations, fathers may not be contacted if their relationship with the mother or the circumstances around the conception of the child are such that any contact with the father may be inappropriate for the best interests of the child (Adoption Act 1998, section 7).

What if the mother refuses to identify the father of the child? Can an adoption proceed?

Yes, adoption may proceed if the father of the child cannot be determined or revealed by the mother. The Board will seek to carry out numerous investigations with the mother in light of possible medical concerns, the father contesting and the welfare of the child. Such adoption may be delayed and/or approved after a period of time.

The Adoption Act 2010 ratifies the Hague Convention on the Protection of Children and provides for the creation of the Adoption Authority as the central authority required under the terms of the Convention to oversee implementation in effecting inter-country adoptions. The Act also deals with miscellaneous issues regarding domestic adoption and ensures the child's best interests are paramount as part of the adoption process. In addition, the Act allows the State to enter into bilateral agreements for inter-country adoptions. The Adoption (Tracing and Information) Bill proposes to provide for an information and tracing service to applicants seeking information about adoptions on a statutory basis. In addition, the thirty-first amendment to the Constitution (the Children's Referendum, passed on 10 November 2012) (under Article 42a) will allow for the adoption of children from parents who have failed to, over a period of time, provide for or consider the best interest of the child. The amendment will also provide, by law, the voluntary placement for adoption and the adoption of any child, including, for the first time, the children of married parents. As part of the reform, the Child and Family Support Agency Bill proposes to establish a child and family support agency for the delivery of child welfare and protection services and the Children First Bill proposes to implement the Programme for Government commitment related to *Children First*, which covers the raising of awareness of child abuse, the recognition and reporting of child abuse, and the management of child safety concerns. Finally, the Children (Amendment) Bill proposes to amalgamate the children's detention schools in the interests of cost and administrative efficiencies and the public interest and to make some technical amendments to improve the workability of certain provisions.

For additional information please contact the Adoption Authority of Ireland on 01-2309300 or at www.aai.gov.ie.

Custody

What is custody, and how does it differ from guardianship?
Custody is essentially the day-to-day care of the child. Married parents have both joint guardianship and joint custody of the child. Non-married mothers are automatic guardians and custodians of their children.

A non-married father may apply for custody, even if he does not have guardianship at the time of application. In some cases, joint custody may be granted to both parents, but this may not be realistic in relation to day-to-day matters. It is essential, therefore, that the best interests and welfare of the child are considered.

What factors are taken into consideration regarding the welfare of the child?
The key issues to be assessed regarding the general welfare of the child (Guardianship of Infants Act 1964, section 3) are as follows:

* Religious
* Moral
* Intellectual
* Physical
* Social and emotional

Other factors to consider are the age, emotional bonding and capacity (mental and physical) of the parents to raise their children. EU Regulation 2201/2003 sets out new rules on jurisdictions (countries where hearings should take place) and recognition and enforcement of judgments (how decisions in one country are recognised in another) in relation to matters of parental responsibility for cases arising on or after 1 March 2005. Such regulations also support cooperation between central authorities between countries, and specific rules on child abduction within the EU.

What should I do if my child is abducted?
Child abduction is the term used to describe a situation where a child is removed from the person who has the

legal right to custody without that person's consent. This also covers situations where the child is not returned to the rightful legal parent on time as agreed or removed from the country without permission.

If you have custody of your child and they are abducted to another EU member state you may apply to that state for the return of the child. Essentially, the purpose of international and EU conventions is to return the child to their main place of residency as soon as possible, or at least ensure the hearing to assess the child's best interests is heard in the child's own residing country. Abductions outside of the EU or to countries that do not recognise international conventions (primarily the Hague Convention, which absorbed the Luxembourg Convention) can be more difficult. The courts of the member state to which the child has been abducted can refuse return of the child on limited grounds only. Such grounds may include where the provision of safeguards in the child's home (member country) are unsatisfactory and there is serious risk to the child.

Parental responsibility includes the rights of custody, access, guardianship and placement of children in foster care. If your child has been internationally abducted you should contact the Central Authority for Child Abduction (within the Department of Justice and Equality) in order to start procedures required in the country to which the child has been abducted. For further details contact the Central Authority for Child Abduction (Lo-call 1890 555 509). If you believe your child is in danger of being abducted contact the Gardaí, who have the power to detain a child if they suspect that the child is about to be removed from the State.

Directive 2009/136/EC, which came into effect on 25 May 2011, requires member states to make every effort to establish a missing children hotline (116000). The Minister for Children and Youth Affairs has committed to the establishment of the hotline in 2013.

Access

My former partner denies me access to our child. What can I do?

The courts like to recommend access to children for both parents, even in situations where supervised access may be granted on initial grounds. It is therefore advisable to seek guardianship first, if not already achieved.

The courts (District or Family Courts), in assessing access, take into consideration the best interests of the child and these rights override the interests of the parents, if conflict arises. Access rights may be reassessed at any time due to a change in circumstances, if a change is in the best interests of the child.

How will the change to the Constitution by referendum change the rights of children?

The thirty-first amendment to the Constitution (Article 42a) (the Children's Referendum), will recognise and enshrine the rights of children in law. In addition, regardless of the marital status of the parents, the State will take responsibility for the child(ren) if the parents fail in their duty of care to the child(ren) or where the child(ren) are put at risk. The fundamental purpose of these additional powers provided to the State is to ensure and recognise the best interests of the child.

In addition, the amendment will ensure the best interests of the child will be of paramount consideration in matters of adoption, guardianship, custody or access.

The child's voice and input into any decision (dependent on their age and maturity) will be given fair consideration before any final decisions are made in relation to them.

Our son has a child. He has split up with his former girlfriend and she refuses to allow us access to the child. Is there anything we can do?
Yes. It is feasible to apply for access for grandparents and relatives of the child (achieved through section 9 of the Children Act 1997, which incorporates section 11b of the Guardianship of Infants Act 1964). In assessing each case the courts must assess the needs of the child and possible disruption to the child, the wishes of the guardians and the guardian's relationship to the child. In each case the court must assess how valid the application is before a hearing takes place.

Can I force my former partner to spend time with our child?
No, generally it is not possible to force a parent to take responsibility for their child's upbringing and/or visitation. In some cases the courts have recommended that fathers take an active involvement in their child's upbringing for the best interests of the child.

Maintenance (Non-Married Couples)

What factors are taken into consideration regarding assessing maintenance for my child?
In general, the court decides what maintenance is proper. It therefore takes into consideration the following factors, under section 5(4A) of the Family Law (Maintenance of

Spouses and Children) Act 1976, inserted via the Status of Children Act 1987:

- Income, earning capacity, property and other financial resources of each party and the dependent child(ren) (and/or other children)
- Financial responsibilities of each person – in non-married situations it is generally only the child's needs that are assessed for maintenance, not the former partner's. (This has changed with the passing of the Civil Partnership and Certain Rights and Obligations of Cohabitants Act 2010, discussed later). Therefore, in general, it is a combination between the best interests of the child, and the financial resources available from each of the supporting parents.

The court must assess the minimum requirements of each person and child, the net income of the maintenance payer and the minimum living requirements of both parties (maximum maintenance €150 per week per child and €500 for a spouse/civil partner – District Court). In some cases additional payments can be requested through the court for birth and funeral expenses for a dependent child (maximum €2,000). A parent can also seek special one-off payments (for example, at Christmas time or at the start of the school year).

What rights does my common law wife have and do I have to support her financially if we split?
The Irish law system does not recognise common law husband and wife situations in the main. Common law relationships are recognised in UK law. In Ireland if such relationships come to an end there was no legal obligation

on either party to support the other prior to the passing of the Civil Partnership and Certain Rights and Obligations of Cohabitants Act 2010 and its implementation on 1 January 2011. Under the Civil Partnership and Certain Rights and Obligations of Cohabitants Act 2010, if a relationship comes to an end there will be a legal obligation on each party to support the other (subject to an "opt-out" clause). Under the legislation, cohabitants (same sex or opposite sex) are persons (section 172) who live together as a couple in an intimate and committed relationship and who are not related to each other within the prohibited degrees of relationship or are married to each other or civil partners of each other. Determining factors include:

- The duration of the relationship
- The basis on which the couple live together
- The degree of financial dependence of each adult on the other
- Whether there are dependent children
- Whether one of the adults cares for and supports the children of the other or the children of the couple
- The degree to which they present themselves to others as a couple

For the avoidance of doubt, a relationship does not cease to be an intimate relationship merely because it is no longer sexual in nature.

What does "civil partnership" mean?
The Civil Partnership and Certain Rights and Obligations of Cohabitants Act 2010 (which was implemented on 1 January 2011) now provides for civil partnership between two adults (over eighteen years of age) of the same gender

who wish to register their partnership (in general compliance with the normal notice period for registration of a marriage).

What are the restrictions in terms of "blood links" for civil partners?

The Act allows a civil partnership on the grounds that neither party is within a prohibited degree of relationship, i.e. they are not blood relations or too closely linked under legislation (Deceased Wife's Sister Act 1907 and the Deceased Husband's Widow's Marriage Act 1921) (section 26).

What rights do civil partners now have?

A civil partnership can only be dissolved upon nullity, death of either party or irretrievable breakdown. The Act provides protection in relation to inheritance, pension rights, social welfare, property and taxation. The parties have, in essence, the same or similar rights as parties to a marriage. The Act also recognises relationships registered abroad and provides a redress scheme in the event of a relationship break-up.

What is the time period for eligibility of rights and when does the "clock" start?

The period of a cohabitant relationship is defined as two years living together where the couple are parents of one or more dependent children or five years living together if there are no children. Time period exemptions apply (in defining qualified cohabitants) if:

- One or both of the adults is, or was at the time of the relationship, married to someone else, and

- At the time the relationship ended, an adult who was married had not lived apart from his or her spouse for a period of at least four years during the previous five years

Essentially, one of the cohabitants can seek a claim at the end of the relationship if financial dependency can be proven. The time period is retrospective prior to the introduction of the legislation so all claims may now be eligible (section 206).

Can I "opt out" of my rights?

Cohabitants may decide to opt out of their rights and sign an agreement waiving rights over each other's possessions for the period of their lifetime or after death. This agreement is only valid if both cohabitants have received independent legal advice before entering it or have received legal advice together and have waived independent legal rights and have signed an agreement.

Do I have any rights if my cohabitee dies?

There are no automatic legal entitlements to each other's estate upon the death of either cohabitant. In law, cohabitants are seen as "non-blood" related (Category 4). Only spouses and registered civil partners have a legal share in their spouse's/civil partner's estate upon death. On the death of one cohabitant, the surviving cohabitant may apply for an order for provision from the net estate (section 194). Claims will be ineligible if the relationship ended two years or more before the death (subject to no other orders outstanding). Any claims must be submitted within two years of the time the relationship ended, whether through death or otherwise.

So when can a cohabitee seek a claim?
Essentially, one of the cohabitants can seek a claim at the end of the relationship if financial dependency can be proven. Determining factors include (similar to separating married or civil partnership couples):

- Financial circumstances, needs and obligations of each cohabitant
- Rights and entitlements of any spouse or former spouse, civil partner or former civil partner
- Rights and entitlements of dependent children of a previous relationship of either cohabitant
- Degree of commitment, duration and basis of relationship
- Contributions made by either cohabitant in looking after the home
- Current and future earning capacity of either cohabitant
- Physical or mental disability
- Conduct of either cohabitant

Claims may be in relation to property, maintenance, pension and attachment of earnings.

What requirements are needed to register a civil partnership?
Three months' notice must now be given in person by both parties to any registration office (exemption of three months may be granted by Circuit or High Court order). Special arrangements can be made if either party is ill or lives outside the State. Notice may still be given in writing if required, but you must then attend in person at least five days prior to the ceremony to sign the declaration. A fee of €150 must be paid, and the registrar requires individual proof of identity and your status (single, divorced,

widowed, dissolution or annulment of a previous civil partnership or annulment of a previous marriage). Upon compliance, a Marriage Registration Form (MRF) or a Civil Partnership Registration Form (CPRF) is issued, which you need in order to marry or register a civil partnership The MRF or CPRF form is only valid for six months from the date of issue. If this time period expires, a new form is required.

Can a foreign gay marriage be accepted in Ireland?

The rules and validity of marriage are determined in each country, so if you are getting married abroad it is important to check with the embassy of the relevant country as to its validity. Marriages abroad do not need to be registered in Ireland. In addition, under the new legislation (Civil Partnership and Certain Rights and Obligations of Cohabitants Act 2010, section 5) the Minister may recognise registered foreign relationships. Some countries may require a "Freedom to Marry" certificate; therefore, it is advisable to discuss this matter with the relevant embassy or the Department of Foreign Affairs. Of course, all marriages abroad must comply with the validity and capacity of Irish law or be in compliance with the recognition of civil partnerships in the jurisdiction you register your partnership, if outside Ireland.

Can maintenance orders be reviewed over time if there is a change in circumstances?

Yes, maintenance orders can be reviewed over time dependent on circumstances changing, e.g. a child becoming an adult, changes in the financial circumstances of either party (maintenance-paying or maintenance-receiving person). It would be advisable to ensure a variation order is included in a maintenance agreement (specifically for the maintenance payer), as non-inclusion will not allow the reduction of payment if required.

Can maintenance payments be deducted at source (i.e. from employment or social welfare payments) from parents who are not supporting their children?
At present under the Family Law (Maintenance of Spouses and Children) Act 1976, section 11, an employer must comply with an attachment of earnings order (made by the court), within ten days of receipt. Therefore, in these situations, the employer is responsible for deducting from his/her employee's payment any court order deductions required. The maintenance debtor (person paying the maintenance) must inform the courts in writing within ten days concerning every occasion he leaves or recommences employment, or becomes self-employed (section 14). Therefore in law, the Department of Social Protection could seek court orders to enforce attachment of earnings orders, even in situations where parents are in receipt of social welfare payments only.

I am concerned my former partner will move to another country. Can the maintenance order still be applicable?
Yes, under numerous Acts maintenance orders can be enforced in other countries subject to those countries' jurisdictions. These Acts include the Maintenance Order Act 1974 (for UK claims), which can be administered in the District Court in Ireland), the Jurisdiction of Courts and Enforcement of Judgment (Amendment) Act 2012 (maintenance across EU states) and the Maintenance Act 1994 (countries covered under the New York Convention, primarily members of the United Nations). For enforcement

of EU and international maintenance orders (excluding the UK), it is advisable to contact the Central Authority for Maintenance Recovery in the Department of Justice and Equality (mainrecov@justice.ie or 1890 555 509). International countries covered under the UN Convention on the Recovery Abroad of Maintenance Payments (New York Convention) include the US, and South American, African, Asian and EU countries (subject to some exceptions). Court maintenance agreements heard in one jurisdiction within the EU can be enforced across other EU states under EU legislation by court order with the assistance of the Central Authority for Maintenance Recovery. European enforcement orders, which are uncontested orders and in operation since October 1995, can be enforced in other EU states without a need for court intervention. The International Recovery of Child Support (Hague Convention) Bill proposes to implement the Hague Convention on International Recovery of Child Support and other forms of family maintenance. This will further enhance and support the implementation of international maintenance orders and agreements.

Maintenance payments have not been paid. What can I do?
Previously, breaches of maintenance payments were enforced by the courts by imposing fines and/or imprisonment for such breaches. This was challenged with the recent High Court judgment in the case of *Caroline McCann v Judge of Monaghan District Court and Others* (2009), which ruled as unconstitutional the procedure adopted by the District Court in imposing imprisonment orders against debtors. In the judgment it was stated that the use of imprisonment was in breach of fair procedures

and personal liberties under the Constitution and that there was no jurisdiction to make an order for jail, and therefore revised proper procedure must be followed for all future cases.

The legislation was therefore amended recently with the passing of the Civil Law (Miscellaneous Provisions) Act 2011, section 31 of which states that it shall be a contempt of court to fail to make a payment due. If breached, a judge or the courts will have powers to give notice to the maintenance debtor (person owing the money) of the implication of that breach, which may impose possible fines or a bench warrant for arrest (assuming there is evidence to prove a summons was served) and notice of a further hearing. At the further hearing the maintenance debtor will be advised of the implications of non-attendance at a rescheduled hearing, and advised clearly of the possibility of availing of free legal aid. The judge upon re-hearing the case, considering the facts (if there is a change of circumstance), may consider a number of options, including re-assessment of the maintenance rate (if any factors relating to the original financial assessment have changed), enforcement of an attachment of earnings order (if upon re-assessment there are no fundamental changes in financial circumstances) or, subject to the facts, declaring a breach of court orders (if the order was simply and clearly not complied with and there was no request for a re-assessment of the circumstances). An attachment of earnings order means that deductions may be made directly from the employee's wage or salary through their employer.

In addition, the Fines (Amendment) Bill proposes to provide for attachment of earnings and social welfare payments as an alternative to imprisonment for people who refuse to pay.

Fostering

We are interested in fostering a child. What is the procedure and what are our rights in relation to the child regarding travel and responsibility?

Fostering involves caring for someone else's child in your own home. This may be either short term or long term (this may be agreed in advance with the HSE). Foster parents may be single, married, widowed or same-sex couples, with the only pre-requirement being to ensure a safe, welcoming and loving home for the child.

To be accepted as foster parent(s), an in-depth screening process is carried out by the HSE incorporating all aspects of your life, including medical and police background checks, interviews with your children (if applicable) and non-family references. The assessment process and waiting list may vary. Under the Child Care (Placement of Children in Foster Care) Regulations 1995, training is provided to foster parent(s).

The original or birth parents always remain guardians of the child. Previously, foster parents did not at any stage become guardians of the child. (In a temporary capacity the HSE can become acting guardians for the child.) Since the passing of section 4 of the Child Care (Amendment) Act 2007 in July 2007, foster parents or relatives who have been caring for a child for a continuous period of at least five years may apply to the court for an order which would grant them rights similar to guardianship rights. When a young person reaches the age of sixteen they can consent to their own medical/dental treatment. A fostering allowance is granted to foster parents by the HSE to support the child.

If you have been fostering for more than six months and the mother has voluntarily given up her child and she has been contributing to the child's support you may be eligible to apply for Child Benefit from the seventh month of fostering. If the child was either voluntarily given up and the mother is not supporting the child or the child has been placed in care following a court order, you can apply for Child Benefit from the second month of fostering. The assessment of the mother is considered as primarily mothers are the sole recipients of the Child Benefit payment. Foster parents are advised to submit their Child Benefit claim immediately after a child is placed in their care.

For further information contact your local HSE office or the Irish Foster Care Association at www.ifca.ie.

Can we adopt the child at some stage in the future?

Previously this was generally not feasible unless the child was given up for adoption (this is extremely rare). Only upon adoption does the status of the parents and child change. Upon adoption, the adopted parents become legal guardians of the child and receive full rights and the child is classified in law equal to that of a biological child (for inheritance purposes). The child also becomes a member of the adopting family. In addition, the previous parent loses all legal rights to the child upon adoption.

The thirty-first amendment to the Constitution (under Article 42a) (the Children's Referendum), will allow for the adoption of children whose parents have failed to, over a period of time, provide for or consider the best interests of the child. The amendment will also provide, by law, for the voluntary placement for adoption and the adoption of any child, subject to considering the best interests of the child.

Domestic Violence

I am living with my partner and am worried about my safety in our home. What can I do?
It is important to note whether the parties are married, in a civil partnership or neither, as the avenues and factors to consider may vary depending on the circumstances. It is essential to consider whether you have a proprietary right to the premises, i.e. do you have a joint mortgage/financial interest in the property or are you residing in your partner's property? If you are not married or in a civil partnership you can get a barring order against a violent partner if you have been living together in an intimate and committed relationship for six out of the previous nine months and s/he does not own most or all of the house you are living in. Therefore, if you do not have any financial input into or control of the property it may not be possible to request the owner to be "barred" from the premises. In that situation, it may only be possible to seek a safety order.

If you are married or in a civil partnership, and can show the court that your spouse/civil partner is violent in any way towards you or the children, you can get a barring order against him/her no matter how long you have lived together and even if he/she owns most or all of the house.

When I fear for my safety, it is not physical violence, but more psychological damage and threats. Does this count?
Yes. When the courts assess your situation, they need to consider your safety and welfare. When determining this, they include mental, physical and emotional welfare.

How can I protect myself?

In your situation (non-married and not in a civil partnership), and in the case where you are joint owners, you can apply for a barring order (to the District Court) if you have lived together for at least six of the previous nine months and your partner does not own all of the house you are living in. A barring order compels the other person to leave the premises where you reside and prevents them from molesting, acting or threatening violence, or putting you at risk in or around the place where you live. In exceptional circumstances the court can grant an interim barring order. This is an immediate order requiring the violent person to leave the family home. The barring order may be granted for up to three years (and can be renewed). A protection order may be granted while you await the outcome of an application for a barring order from the court. This protects you from violence, molestation or fear, but does not confer any power to remove the person from the property.

Since August 2011, under the Civil Law (Miscellaneous Provisions) Act 2011, section 60, if you are not married or in a civil partnership you can get a safety order against a violent partner (same sex or opposite sex) if you are living together in an intimate and committed relationship. You can also get a safety order against a person with whom you have had a child but you are not living with or if have never lived with the person.

In the situation where you are residing with your partner and have no greater legal share, i.e. you own a smaller proportion of the property, you can apply for a safety order. A safety order directs the other person not to molest, act or threaten to use violence, or put you in a state of fear in or around the place where you live. A safety order can be granted by the District Court for a period of five years (renewable). To be eligible for a safety order you must have resided together for six of the previous twelve months.

The difference between a barring order, protection order and safety order, therefore, is that a barring order can "bar" a person from a premises if a greater property interest is present; a protection order can be granted as an interim measure while you await a review of a barring order (no barring powers but protection against violence); and a safety order provides a long-term order for your safety (no barring powers).

I am married and afraid for my safety. How does the procedure differ from that which applies to non-married couples?
A spouse or civil partner can apply for a barring order regardless of time or property interest (as the Family Home Protection Act 1976 applies). Therefore, in your situation, you can apply for a barring order and/or a safety order.

Do I need to apply for both or does the judge decide which is best for me?
It may be important to apply for both because then the court can decide which is most appropriate. If you only apply for one order (barring or safety), the court cannot grant the other order without it being submitted at the time of application.

I am at serious immediate risk. What can I do?
An interim barring order is an application to the court for protection when one of the parties is at immediate

or serious risk of harm and a protection order (as above) would be unsuitable to remove the other party.

A person could, in the past, be granted such an order without the other person knowing or having notice of such an application (Domestic Violence Act 1996). As you can understand, this is against the normal principles of natural justice. Such orders were called *ex parte* orders. Interim orders are still valid but a minor change (Domestic Violence Amendment Act 2002) has been made to restrict an *ex parte* order to a maximum of eight working days and all evidence must be given to the person the order is taken against as soon as possible.

What powers do these Acts truly have? Can the Gardaí enforce them?

These powers (orders from the court) are given to the Gardaí in your local area. The Gardaí can arrest a person, without the need for a warrant, if the orders are broken. Domestic violence assaults are a criminal matter and can be prosecuted. The Gardaí can also force entry into premises and arrest a person if there is suspicion or evidence that an assault has taken place or will take place.

I am concerned about my eldest son; he is very aggressive towards me. Can I do anything?

Yes, it may be possible to commence either a safety or even a barring order against him. Your son must not be a dependent child, i.e. must be over eighteen. The same procedure as above applies and you go through your local District Court.

Domestic Violence Against Children

I am concerned about the safety of a young neighbour child. What can I do?
Child abuse is a very serious concern. Such abuse may be in the form of neglect or emotional, physical or sexual abuse. When assessing the situation, it is important to take a fully objective view of the case and truly question your concerns in a realistic and open manner.

If, upon reflection, you feel there is a real and substantial risk to a child, you should report the issue to your local social worker in the HSE, or, if there is urgent, immediate danger, contact the Gardaí.

What if I get the report wrong? What are the implications for me?
There are no implications for you, as an individual, if you report your concerns, presuming there was no clear malicious intent and the report was genuine (you are protected under the Protections for Persons Reporting Child Abuse Act 1998). In most cases the HSE or the Gardaí will assess the report before acting on it.

I am an employee and am worried about the safety of a client's child who visited us at work. Will I get in trouble if I report this?
No, under the Protections for Persons Reporting Child Abuse Act 1998, with specific reference to section 4, employees and their employers are protected from penalisation in reporting child abuse, presuming the assessment was reasonable and in good faith, and there was no clear

malicious intent. An employee is also protected from dismissal by an employer, on the grounds that the employee acted in good faith in the situation by contacting the relevant organisation (Gardaí or HSE).

What can the Gardaí or HSE do in these situations?

The Child Care Act 1991 gives powers to the Gardaí to take immediate action in urgent and emergency situations. The Gardaí can remove a child and enter a house without a warrant. In such cases, the Gardaí present the child to the HSE, who assess the situation.

The HSE can apply to the courts for a care order if there is immediate risk and serious concern for the welfare of the child. This allows it to take custody of the child for a period of time. If the courts do not deem this necessary, but they are concerned for the child's welfare, they may grant a supervision order, which allows the HSE to visit the child in their home and ascertain if they are being ill-treated.

What about children who are homeless or have run away?

The HSE, if they become aware of a child lost or abandoned, must try to reunite the child with his/her parent(s), if it is in the child's best interests. If this is not suitable or if the parents themselves have no accommodation, the HSE will take appropriate steps. The HSE may make accommodation available to the child or consider taking the child into care (Child Care Act 1991, section 5).

Wills and Inheritance

Why is it important to make a will?

If you die and you have made a will, it is clear how you wish your assets to be divided. This is important if you want to specify particular items, property or specific amounts of money should go to different people or organisations. This is not to say that you can refuse or bypass legal entitlements (to your spouse/civil partner) in your will, which are protected in the Succession Act 1965 (legal right shares for spouse/civil partner).

When you die and have a will in place, you are known to have died "testate". When you die without having a will, you are known to have died "intestate". The Succession Act 1965 clearly dictates the division of assets in order of relationship to the deceased person. If no living relation exists after your death, your assets go the State.

Do I need to go to a solicitor to make a will?
No, it is not necessary to go to a solicitor to make a will. Standard samples of wills are available from stationery shops, or alternatively you can write your own. If in doubt about the complexity of specific wills, legal advice should be sought.

So what are the essential elements of a valid will?
The person making the will must have full capacity, i.e. must be of sound mind and character and be over eighteen years old. If this is contested in the future, the burden of proof is on the person contesting it to prove otherwise.

A will must be in writing (not on DVD, video, cassette or e-mail). It must be signed and dated at the very bottom of the document by the person making the will. The witnesses do not have to see the content of the document; they need only see the person signing the document. Two independent witnesses must see the document being signed. Such witnesses must not gain from the will. If the witnesses end up financially gaining from the will, the will still remains valid, but they lose their entitlements.

If a will does not cover the distribution of all property or assets, the remaining asset distribution may be by means of partial intestacy (natural succession). If a will is not valid, the rule of intestacy applies (as if there was no will, i.e. natural succession).

In legal terms, a man making a will is known as a "testator" and a woman is known as a "testatrix".

What is a "living will"? Is it valid?

A "living will" is a document stating when medical treatment should stop when the person becomes mentally incapable. These may be valid in Ireland, although there have been no legal challenges to date. Here, this is purely a medical practitioner's decision, although the new Advance Healthcare Decisions Bill proposes to allow people to leave instructions, either written or verbal, on treatment they wish to receive in the event of an accident or incapacitating illness, and to nominate another person, a healthcare proxy, to carry out their wishes. It will also allow people to refuse life-saving treatment, such as a blood transfusion, for religious reasons.

My father wrote a will and had two valid witnesses, but one of the witnesses was me (his son) and I am to gain from his will. My father died last week and my brother told me I will not gain anything from his will. Is this true?

Yes, unfortunately this is true in this situation. Beneficiaries (people who gain from a will) can be seen as a valid witness but will not be entitled to any of the estate. In this case the will is seen as valid (two independent witnesses), but as one of the witnesses was you, his son, you lose any legal right to benefit from that will. Therefore it is not advisable for any proposed beneficiaries of your estate to be a witness to your will. It is advisable to have two totally independent persons witness your will, people who will not gain in any way whatsoever from your future estate or the wishes of your will.

Can I change a will and is there a limit to the number of times I can do this?

It is presumed any changes to the original will that are not subsequently signed and witnessed are invalid. You can change or destroy a will, even the original, but every alteration must be signed and witnessed. It is advisable, therefore, to write another will (revoking the first or subsequent will), or add an additional page(s) to the original (codicil or supplement).

In changing the will, the person must state the new will is the final will (revoke the first or subsequent). Alternatively, you can destroy the original will if the new will states all previous wills are cancelled (revoked).

What if the last will cannot be found after a person's death?

It is advisable to keep your will in safekeeping and inform either the executor (person who carries out the wishes of the deceased) or another person where it is kept.

If a final (subsequent) will is lost, the court may try to reassess its contents, but the concern would be that the exact nature and content of the new will may not be fully reconstructed. Also, concerns may be raised regarding the destruction of the new will by a certain party. Therefore, in summary, the only valid will to exist may be the original one, and therefore may have to be executed in full.

I wrote a will when I was single. I have just gotten married. Is the will still valid?

No, a will changes upon marriage/civil partnership and becomes null and void, as marriage/civil partnership changes the legal right share of the spouse/civil partner.

I am separated from my wife. Is she still my spouse for inheritance purposes?

A spouse is still a spouse upon separation or judicial separation. Clauses may be written into the separation agreement excluding the other party from access to inheritance, but they may be challenged. Divorce or dissolution of a civil partnership is the only legal proceeding that removes the legal right share of a spouse/civil partner (even in such a situation limited exceptions may apply).

Do I have to appoint an executor at the time of writing a will? What if they die before me?

No, you do not have to appoint an executor at the time of writing the will, although it is advisable, as complications and additional costs may be incurred. If the executor dies before the person making the will, any other person who will gain (beneficiary) from the will can be granted administration through an application to probate.

What does an executor or administrator do?

The executor or administrator carries out the wishes of the deceased (via their will). The executor must be over eighteen years old and must not suffer from any disability (physical or mental) that prevents them from carrying out the duties of an executor). Firstly, the executor or administrator must prove a valid will exists by providing a copy to the probate office and seeking a grant of representation through the probate office to carry out the administration of the will.

All assets are frozen after death (except joint accounts, if one party is still living). The executor or administrator must ensure any outstanding debts are paid off as soon as possible after the person has died. Any property or assets lie in the control of the executor or administrator during such procedures and they can sell any assets to release equity (monetary value) to clear debts and distribute gains among the beneficiaries (people who inherit) of the will. In some cases a specific item can be given in lieu of the value of such inheritance. The executor or administrator should ensure any assets are preserved and protected before distribution.

What if you are unhappy with the executor or administrator? Can you change them?
Yes, it may be possible to request a change of administrator or executor if they have not proceeded with such actions within a twelve-month period, declined the duties or did not comply exactly with the distribution of the estate as stated in the will or distribute the estate in compliance with the legal right share under the legislation. An application can be made to the court to request a new administrator via a grant of representation.

What is probate and should it be used in all cases, even if no will exists?
An application for a grant of probate must be made to the probate office in the area in which the person died. The application is made by the executor or administrator and the following documents are forwarded (as required):

- Notice of application – this ensures no second application is made
- Copy of will – valid legible copy and any additional documents (codicils)
- Oath of executor – a written statement (oath) by the executor signed by a practising solicitor or Commissioner for Oaths to agree to pay all outstanding debts
- Death certificate
- Revenue affidavit – document including all assets and liabilities (monies due) at the time of death of the person. All beneficiaries (people who will gain from the will) must also sign a document stating all gifts received by them.

Other documentation may be required depending on the validity of the will. A grant of probate should be carried out in all situations regardless of whether there is a will (testate) or no will (intestate) in place.

Does the probate application have to be done by a solicitor?

No, not necessarily. The grant of probate can be carried out by any person acting as executor or administrator. The probate office will assist you in the process. In complicated situations, or if such action has been commenced by a solicitor, it may not be possible to execute the grant of probate by yourself.

Is probate tax still in existence?

No, probate tax was abolished in relation to any deaths after 6 December 2000.

What if I want to oppose a grant of probate – what can I do?
You must submit an application (caveat) to the probate office. A copy will be sent to the person who originally made the application. The application can remain in place for six months. After that, it would then need to be investigated for clarification.

What if the person dies in debt?
It is important to assess fully all assets at the time of death, even if the person was insolvent (had no cash or reserves). The sequence of priorities is laid down, including (in the following order):

- Funeral costs
- Secured creditors (mortgage providers)
- Rates or taxes
- Wages or salaries (if an employer)

Therefore any outstanding creditors can only reclaim costs from the estate remaining. Relatives bear no personal liability for any debts over and above the assets of the estate.

What if the person wanted to defraud their spouse/civil partner or children of their inheritances?
If a person has no valid will they cannot defraud their spouse/civil partner or children of their legal right share. Under section 121 of the Succession Act 1965, the courts can assess any gifts from the person's (testator's or testatrix's) estate for a period of three years prior to their death.

If these gifts were made to defraud or reduce the share of their spouse/civil partner or children, they can be taken into consideration when assessing the person's estate.

My husband died recently and he did not leave me anything in his will. What is my legal situation?
The will of a deceased spouse/civil partner cannot ignore the legal entitlement of the surviving spouse/civil partner. In this instance the surviving spouse/civil partner is entitled to (at least) half of the estate if there are no children and a minimum one-third if there are children. You can request that the property be sold to release your legal right share.

If in the will you are given a gift, you have the choice to accept the gift or your legal right share, whichever is the greater, but you must inform the executor or administrator of your choice. You may also be able to accept property instead of cash or equity, depending on the property's value. If the property is worth more than you are entitled to, you could pay the balance into the estate to be divided appropriately among the other beneficiaries. In some cases this value may be assessed by the courts, or even reduced depending on the factors of the case.

My mother died recently and did not leave us anything in her will. Is this possible?
There is no automatic entitlement for children regarding their legal right share if there is a valid will which clearly excludes them from any inheritance. The only possibility would be to contest the will on grounds of a section 117 application. Such an application must be made within six months of the commencement of representation of the deceased's estate.

A section 117 application is required to prove that such children did not have proper provision during their lifetime. Factors to consider include:

- The number of children, their ages and position in the family (i.e. eldest, youngest, etc.)
- The means of the deceased parent
- Age of the applicant child(ren) (children may be of adult age, adopted or born outside marriage)
- A child's financial situation, prospects, educational access and financial provision made during his/her life by the parent
- Moral duty of parent and child to each other and/or third parties

In assessing the application the courts must decide not what an average parent would have done, but specifically what a fair and just parent would have done.

My wife died suddenly and she did not have a will. What is my legal position?

Firstly, we must consider if there are any children. If there are children, you will get two-thirds of her estate and the children receive one-third. If there are no children, you will receive the whole estate. If it is a case that your son or daughter is deceased, that son or daughter's children (i.e. your grandchildren) receive your son or daughter's share proportionately.

Example

Mary was married to Robert. They had three children – Shane, Claire and Susan. Shane had two children (Robbie and Caroline), Claire has no children and Susan has three children (Tom, John and Brian). Shane died three years ago. Mary died last week but did not have a will. How is the estate divided?

In this situation, Robert, as spouse, receives two-thirds of the estate. The three children receive one-third of the estate divided three ways (one-ninth each). As Shane is dead, his children (Mary's grandchildren) divide his share equally (so they get one-eighteenth each). Tom, John and Brian do not receive any share as Susan (their mother) is still alive and she receives a share of one-ninth of the estate.

My cousin died without making a will. I am not sure if I am the only living relative. Am I entitled to her estate? What should I do?

Firstly, it is important to ask the following questions, in order of sequence, to understand fully the rule of natural succession:

- Was she married/in a civil partnership?
- Did she have any children?
- Are her parents alive?
- Did she have any brothers or sisters and did they have any children?
- Are her grandparents still alive?
- Are there any aunts or uncles alive?
- Are there any great-grandparents alive?
- Are there any grandnephews, grandnieces, grandaunts, granduncles or first cousins alive?

It may be advisable to draw a family tree starting with the deceased. It is important to determine the degree (layers) of relationship between the deceased and living relatives.

The person with the lowest degree of relationship (i.e. the closest relationship) to the deceased will inherit. If two relatives of equal degree exist, the sequence above gives priority. If you believe you are the only surviving relative, you should contact the Probate Office on 01-8886174 or e-mail probategeneraloffice@courts.ie.

My mother married 30 years ago. Her first husband died 20 years ago; during their marriage they had three children. She later remarried and had four children with her current husband. He never officially adopted her children from her first marriage, as at that time it was too expensive. Her second husband died last week without a will. Do her children from her first marriage have any inheritance?

The children from the first marriage, although raised by the second husband as his children, have no direct entitlement to his succession, as they were not officially adopted at that time. Therefore, in this situation, his wife is entitled to two-thirds of his estate and the children from his marriage are entitled to one-third between them.

Children when adopted and/or born outside marriage have the same entitlement as children naturally born or born within marriage.

What is Capital Acquisitions Tax and how does it apply after death?

Capital Acquisitions Tax (CAT) is a combination of both Inheritance Tax (gifts left after a person dies) and Gift Tax (amounts of money given to other parties during the deceased's life). The important factors to consider are what the relationship was between the giver and receiver, when the gifts were given and how much was given both before and after death.

CAT is a self-assessment tax chargeable at 33 per cent (as laid out in Budget 2013) above the thresholds. Payments may be made by instalments through prior agreement with Revenue. Interest is charged if this not paid within four months. Interest is charged at 0.0322 per cent per day (11.75 per cent per annum).

What are the thresholds for Gift or Inheritance Tax?

Inheritance from a spouse/civil partner is exempt from Inheritance Tax. The following thresholds are applicable:

* Category 1 – gifts or inheritances between spouses/civil partners are not taxable
* Category 2 – gifts or inheritances from parents to children (and vice versa) and grandchildren (under eighteen) if the parent is deceased. This also includes foster children (since 6 December 2000) cared for for a period of at least five years, if the child is under eighteen years – €225,000 (since 5 December 2012)
* Category 3 – gifts or inheritances between brothers, sisters, uncles, aunts, nephews, nieces, grandchildren and grandparents – €30,150 (since 5 December 2012)
* Category 4 – gifts or inheritances between others (not blood related) – €15,075 (since 5 December 2012)

Non-married couples would fall into Category 4, as their relationship is not seen as "blood-related or spouse/civil partner".

It is also important to consider all gifts received by a specified person from 5 December 1991 to date. Such dates are re-assessed by Revenue on a periodic basis, as the inheritance payment is an accumulative amount for the total period since 1991 within each separate category above. Tax is applicable on amounts over and above the thresholds. Self-assessment tax returns (Form IT38, available from www.revenue.ie) should be completed if the value of the inheritance is within 80 per cent of the maximum threshold. The pay and file deadline has been brought forward from 31 October to 30 September each year (Finance Act 2011).

What is the situation with the family home when someone dies?

When the family home is held in a joint tenancy (by spouses or civil partners), the surviving spouse or civil partner automatically inherits. In other cases no Capital Acquisitions Tax is applicable on an inheritance of a family home if:

• The person receiving the property lived in the house for three years prior to the transfer, and
• The person receiving the property has no interest in other residential (home) properties, and
• The person receiving the property intends to live at the property for a further six years (this is exempt if they are over 55) (other requirements may apply)

Other complications may arise regarding the legal ownership of the property, the contents of a will (if in existence), the legal right share of the beneficiary, intestacy entitlements (where there is no will), the relationship (blood or otherwise) with the deceased and the market value of the property at the time of transfer or valuation.

I want to give our family home to my son before I die. Will I, or my son, be liable for Capital Acquisitions Tax?
We must consider the market value of the property at the time of sale or transfer. All gifts or inheritances have to be assessed at the market value at the time of transfer or valuation date. In this situation, if the market value is lower than the threshold and your son had not received any other gifts from you, the parent, since 5 December 1991, no Capital Acquisitions Tax may be applicable.

If other gifts had been given from 5 December 1991 to date within the same category, i.e. parent to child, the total amount is aggregated (added together) and the excess of the threshold is chargeable at 33 per cent (as laid out in Budget 2013). The tax amount is payable within four months of the transfer or valuation date.

Alternatively, your son may be eligible for an exemption from CAT if (as we have seen above) he can comply with the requirements of:

- Having lived at the address for the previous three years, and
- Having no other residential property, and
- Planning to live at the address for a further six years

In relation to the giver of the gift, no taxes are applicable.

Are there any exemptions regarding Capital Acquisitions Tax?
Yes, some of the following are examples of where exemptions apply:

- The first €3,000 of gifts from one donor (excluding inheritance)
- Lottery winnings (exemption applies only to the person receiving the gift, which is why it is important)
- Payments made during a lifetime for normal costs, e.g. education
- Specific gifts or inheritances for medical expenses or costs for permanently disabled persons

Ward of Court

I am worried about my mother's mental health, and if she is of sound mind in making financial decisions. What can you recommend?
You may wish to consider making your mother a "ward of court". This is required when a person is unable to manage their affairs due to a mental incapacity (this may also be applicable to persons under eighteen years of age). The court will be required to ensure the person is of unsound mind and incapable of managing their own affairs. You will be required to make a petition to the High Court, with proof from two doctors. For further information contact the Office of the Ward of Court or check www.courts.ie.

The new Mental Capacity Bill proposes to replace the "ward of court" and "enduring power of attorney" system. In addition, it proposes to reform the law on mental capacity, taking into account the Law Reform Commission's report on *Vulnerable Adults and the Law*. An enduring power of attorney is a legal document in which you give another person the power to make decisions on your behalf if you ever lose the capacity in the future to make decisions yourself. The new Bill proposes to consider the appointment of a "guardian" in the best interests of the person. In addition, the Bill proposes to examine the necessary interventions as they arise, the person's "best interests" and their capacity to understand. Hearings will be held in private with all relevant parties. There are no developments or updates on the progress of the Bill.

CHAPTER 4

Marriage and Civil Partnership

Engagements

We are an engaged couple, and we bought a house together. Our relationship is going through a difficult time and we may split up. If we do split up, how will the courts assess us?

Property purchased by a couple whose engagement has ended is protected under family law legislation as if the couple were married (Family Law Act 1981, section 5; Family Law Act 1995, section 36; and Family Law (Divorce) Act 1996, section 44), presuming both parties have a beneficial (financial) interest in the property. This only relates to property purchases during the engagement, and not afterwards.

If we split up after getting engaged, what happens to the engagement presents?

When people give presents to an engaged couple, there is a presumption under law (Family Law Act 1981, section 3) that if the marriage does not take place or the engagement is terminated the donor (the person giving the present) is entitled to the present back. In the case of an engagement ring, it is also presumed under law (section 4) that the ring will be returned if the engagement is terminated, although if the person who gave the ring dies, there is no unconditional return required. Section 7 of the Family Law Act 1981 allows a fiancé(e) to seek a remedy for costs that were incurred in preparation for the marriage. A claim must be submitted within three years of the termination of the engagement (section 9).

There is no clear provision or amendment in the Civil Partnership and Certain Rights and Obligations of Cohabitants Act 2010 in relation to the rights of civil partners prior to the registration of the relationship.

Preparation for Marriage/Civil Partnership

Marriage/Civil Partnership Registration

So what are the basic requirements of marriage/civil partnership?
You must:

- Be aged 18 years or older (if under 18 you require a court exemption). Parental consent is no longer required.
- Be of the opposite sex for marriage or of the same sex to register a civil partnership
- Have a capacity to marry/register a civil partnership with each other (i.e. understand the commitment and implications of the marriage/civil partnership)
- Be free to consent to marriage/civil partnership (i.e. not be currently married or in a civil partnership)
- Comply with the formal notification requirements, and

- Not be related by blood, marriage or civil partnership to a degree prohibited by law. Section 26 of the Civil Partnership and Certain Rights and Obligations of Cohabitants Act 2010 sets down the prohibited degrees of relationships for both male and female civil partners. The Deserted Wife's Sister Act 1907 and Deceased Husband's Widow's Marriage Act 1921 set down the restriction of prohibited degrees for married (opposite-sex) couples. There is no legal restriction on the marriage of first cousins but you are restricted from marrying your half-brother or half-sister.

You will also need to visit the registrar in person and bring the following information/documentation (for both parties) at least three months before the proposed date of marriage/registration of civil partnership:

- Passport
- Birth certificates and PPS numbers
- If divorced a decree of divorce is required; if you were previously in a civil partnership a dissolution of civil partnership certificate is required
- If widowed/a surviving civil partner, a death certificate and previous marriage certificate/civil registration certificate is required
- Whether you propose to have a civil or religious ceremony and the name of the solemniser
- Intended date and location of marriage/registration of civil partnership
- Names and dates of birth of both proposed witnesses
- Proof of annulment (nullity of previous marriage or registered civil partnership) if applicable
- Fee of €150

Postal applications can be made with the prior approval of the registrar. The three-month notice requirement will still, of course, need to be complied with for postal applications. An exemption can be made to the registrar to waive the three months' notice but only with the provision of a court order. Court orders tend only be granted in circumstances due to serious medical conditions of one or both of the parties or if there is "good reason" as approved by the Court and is in the best interest of the parties. You will also have to sign a declaration stating that there is no legal restriction to you marrying/registering a civil partnership. If you did not meet the registrar in person at an earlier point and sign the declaration, you must meet the registrar at least five days before the wedding/registration of civil partnership to sign this declaration.

In summary, the traditional definition of marriage was that of "the voluntary union for life, of one man and one woman, to the exclusion of all others" and as per previous legislation under the Marriages (Ireland) Act 1844 and Matrimonial Causes and Marriage Law (Ireland) Amendment Act 1870 and as amended by the Marriage Act 1972. With the passing of the Civil Partnership and Certain Rights and Obligations of Cohabitants Act 2010 this now allows for the registration and recognition of civil partners of the same sex and granting, in the main, the same or similar rights to that of married couples to couples in civil partnership.

This legislation was developed separately as there was concern that Article 41 of the Constitution (which says "the State recognises the Family as the natural primary and fundamental unit group of Society, and as a moral institution possessing inalienable and imprescriptible rights, antecedent and superior to all positive law") and the rights of the "family" under the Constitution would have been undermined by granting similar rights to same-sex couples without legislative change or alternatively without a referendum to change Article 41. Traditionally, the Constitution's understanding of Article 41 interpreted the "family" as that of a married family of opposite sex.

In addition, the Civil Partnership and Certain Rights and Obligations of Cohabitants Act 2010 legislated for the provision of the break-up of cohabiting couples (both same sex and opposite sex) to seek financial provision or redress, subject to a number of eligibility criteria and financial assessment. This legislation does not introduce entitlements to "common law" rights for partners (same and opposite sex) similar to those in the UK, where rights are granted depending upon the length of the relationship.

I believe the procedure in giving notice to marry has changed. I also heard we can pick a venue where we want to get married. Is this true, and what is the new procedure?
Since 5 November 2007 (as part of the Civil Registration Act 2004) changes have been implemented regarding the procedure and possible venue of marriage. Three months' notice must now be given in person by both parties to any registration office (exemption of three months may be granted by Circuit or High Court order). Special arrangements can be made if either party is ill or lives outside the State. Notice may still be given in writing if required, but you must then attend in person at least five days prior to the ceremony to sign the declaration. A fee of €150 must be paid, and the registrar requires individual proof of identity and your status (single, divorced or widowed). Upon compliance, a Marriage Registration Form (MRF) is issued, which allows you to marry. Without this form you

cannot get married. The MRF form is only valid for six months from the date of issue. If this time period expires, a new form is required.

A venue for the marriage must be in public and agreed by both parties and the person solemnising the marriage. The solemniser must ensure both parties are present, both witnesses are over eighteen years of age, and all the parties are aware of the nature and declaration of marriage. The Civil Registration (Amendment) Bill proposes to amend the Civil Registration Act 2004 to extend the categories that are currently permitted to legally solemnise marriages to include nominees of other bodies (including the Humanist Association of Ireland). In addition, the Civil Registration (Amendment) (No 2) Bill, which is scheduled to be published in 2013, proposes to provide for further amendments to the Civil Registration Act 2004 in relation to the registration of births and deaths, to validate embassy marriages/civil partnerships, to prevent marriages of convenience and to make a number of other amendments.

You can get married either by religious ceremony or civil ceremony. Venues for civil ceremonies must be pre-approved by the registrar and must be in a public place. Religious ceremonies must be approved by religious denominations. You cannot renew your vows in a civil ceremony (as you can only marry the same person once) but you may wish to have a "church blessing". The venue must also be approved by the registrar (using guidelines provided under the Civil Registration Act 2004). An interpreter must be provided where any of the parties (including witnesses) do not have sufficient knowledge of the language to understand. This cost must be arranged by the couple at their own expense. In addition, there may be costs incurred for travel for the registrar subject to the location/venue of the marriage/registration of civil partnership. Under the Social Welfare (Miscellaneous Provisions) Act 2009 the functions of the General Register Office has transferred from the Minister for Health and Children to the Minister for Social Protection. For further information please check www.groireland.ie.

The rules and validity of marriages/civil partnerships abroad are determined in each country. It is important to check with the embassy of the country in which you plan to marry/register a civil partnership as to its validity. Marriages/civil partnerships abroad do not need to be registered in Ireland (as long as they comply with the requirements). Section 5 of the Civil Partnership and Certain Rights and Obligations of Cohabitants Act 2010 sets down the recognition of registered foreign relationships and it states legal relationships must be exclusive in nature, permanent unless dissolvable through the courts, registered under the relevant jurisdiction and in the opinion of the Minister for Justice, Equality and Defence is sufficient to indicate that the relationship would be treated comparably to a civil partnership. A list of recognised jurisdictions of civil partnerships is available from www.justice.ie. Some countries may require a "Freedom to Marry" certificate; therefore it is advisable to discuss this matter with the relevant embassy or the Department of Foreign Affairs. Of course, all marriages abroad must comply with the validity and capacity of Irish law.

Is the procedure any different for registering a civil partnership? Can a registrar refuse to register our civil partnership?
In essence, under Part 7a (section 59) of the Civil Partnership and Certain Rights and Obligations of Cohabitants

Act 2010 the process is the same, with the provision of a Civil Partnership Registration Form (CPRF) in place of the MRF. Registrars who refuse or without reasonable cause fail to provide a civil partnership form to the intended civil partners shall be classed as committing an offence under section 22(9a) of the Act.

Prenuptial Agreements

What is a prenuptial agreement and are they valid in Irish law?

A prenuptial agreement is an agreement made between two parties prior to marriage, with reference to property or assets in the event of marriage breakup. Before the introduction of the Family Law Divorce Act 1996, such agreements were seen not to be applicable.

With reference to the role of the courts regarding divorce, the court must be satisfied that such provisions have proper regard to the circumstances of the case. Therefore prenuptial agreements can now be seen as a factor in the overall consideration, subject to both parties having received independent legal advice before signing the agreement, and assuming neither party was under duress to sign the document. However, prenuptials cannot generally take into consideration the needs of future children prior to marriage.

The courts, therefore, have discretion to consider all factors applicable to the case in the best interests of all. Section 83 of the Civil Partnership and Certain Rights and Obligations of Cohabitants Act 2010 also sets down an amendment to allow for the possibility to waive any legal rights of succession prior to the registration of or during the lifetime of the civil partnership, assuming both parties agree a contract in writing. Section 202 waives any right to maintenance or financial support to cohabiting couples (same or opposite sex) as long as both parties receive independent legal advice and are not under duress to sign an agreement. The courts have the final decision as to the validity of this agreement.

Mediation

What is the Family Mediation Service?
The Family Mediation Service is a free service that provides an independent opportunity for both parties to come together and facilitate mutual agreement of issues of separation (for married/civil partnership couples) and shared parenting (for non-married/civil partnership couples), including for same-sex couples. Section 111 of the Civil Partnership and Certain Rights and Obligations of Cohabitants Act 2010 gives powers to the courts to seek an adjournment in a case of dissolution of a civil partnership at any time to seek mediation to try to either reconcile or reach agreement for dissolution (although there is no compulsion to seek mediation for civil partners as there is for married couples). Section 138 states that the costs of mediation are at the discretion of the courts, but as stated earlier mediation is free through the Family Mediation Service. Section 193 of the Act also recommends mediation for cohabiting couples (same and opposite sex). The Family Mediation Service was previously available from the Department of Social Protection. In November 2011, it was transferred to the Legal Aid Board.

The service is available nationwide, but both parties must be independently willing to come to the table to try to facilitate agreement. The process involves all parties (including dependent children if required), via numerous consultations, developing a written framework for agreement, which hopefully can be "rubber-stamped" by each party's legal representation to develop the basis of a separation agreement. For non-married/civil partnership couples, such agreements can be brought to the attention of the court and considered to be implemented via a court order.

What is this new method called collaborative practice?

Collaborative practice is a new way of resolving family law matters including divorce, separation, dissolution of registered civil partnerships and parenting disputes. This. new method is beneficial as it is a face-to-face agreement between both persons (and their respective legal teams) to resolve matters without going to court. Collaborative lawyers are specially trained, and will not represent you if, in the breakdown of discussions, the matter goes to court. In essence, this is the last approach prior to court intervention.

Separation Agreements

What is the difference between a separation agreement and a judicial separation?

A separation agreement is an agreement between a married couple (normally facilitated by a mediator or solicitor) regarding all issues in relation to the separation, i.e. property, maintenance, etc. This is agreed between the parties (or solicitors) formally and in writing. Such agreements may exclude the future division of assets, if agreed by both parties. (This may be excluded by the courts in the case of divorce, i.e. divorce is the final assessment of assets. In this situation the judge is the final independent assessor of needs at that time and no parties can pre-plan the division or non-division of assets without the final assessment process being ratified.)

A judicial separation is an agreement set down by the courts after both parties are heard. A judicial separation has additional powers, including pension adjustment orders, and has a more formal and structured legal approach, in compliance with the Judicial Separation and Family Law Reform Act 1989. On average a judicial separation is more expensive, as legal representation in court is required by both parties (unless parties are eligible for civil legal aid).

Section 110 of the Civil Partnership and Certain Rights and Obligations of Cohabitants Act 2010 can allow for the dissolution of a registered civil partnership by court order; however this is similar to divorce rather than judicial separation, and is discussed in more detail in the section on divorce below.

Section 173 of the Act also considers proper provision, through the courts, for dependent qualified cohabitants. A dependent qualified cohabitant is defined as one of two adults (same or opposite sex) who live together as a couple in an intimate and committed relationship. This is defined as a couple with dependent children who have lived together for two years or more or a couple without children who have lived together for five years or more. For clarity purposes, the dependent relationship does not cease to be an intimate relationship if it no longer sexual in nature (section 172(3)). In addition, the other factors a court must consider is the basis on which the couple lived together, the degree of financial dependency, the degree and nature of any financial arrangements regarding property, any dependent children, the caring and support of children and the degree to which the adults presented themselves to others as a couple.

What are the benefits of either approach – separation agreement or judicial separation?

There is no outstanding benefit to either approach other than that a separation agreement may be less expensive (or facilitated via family mediation), less formal (no courts are required), less confrontational and both parties can continue to live separate lives even if they decide not to proceed with divorce.

A judicial separation is a more formalised procedure including amendments for pension adjustment orders (if applicable) for both married and registered civil partnership couples and dependent qualified cohabitants and may be more suitable if both parties cannot agree arrangements for separation informally or formally.

The Family Law Bill makes provision for pension adjustment orders via a separation agreement and not solely through a judicial separation (via the courts). The Bill also proposes to make further reforms in the family law area. This Bill has been on the Government legislative programme since 2006 and is proposed to be published in 2013.

In both cases, parties still remain spouses (married opposite-sex couples) and are restricted in their right to remarry, although dissolutions of civil partnerships allow the former civil partners to remarry/form new civil partnerships. Both spouses (married opposite-sex couples) may also have access to future earnings, windfalls or succession if either party dies or receives financial gifts after such agreements have been made and before either party proceeds with divorce. Clauses may be inserted to remove future windfalls or financial gain, except the right to receive benefits upon death (succession), either with or without a will, as both parties are still spouses. As stated previously, registered civil partners have the same rights as married couples when it comes to inheritance, although provision can be made by written agreement to waive any rights to future inheritance. Dissolution of a registered civil partnership also removes any future rights to succession. Section 194 of the Civil Partnership and Certain Rights and Obligations of Cohabitants Act 2010 allows a dependent qualified cohabitant to apply after death (no longer than six months after the death) for a financial provision from the net estate.

As divorce or judicial separation is an assessment or reassessment of assets at the time of being carried out, a previous separation agreement may be included in the assessment, but the courts may alter any prior agreements to ensure an up-to-date assessment of needs and incorporate any changes in the circumstances of either party. The same also applies upon the dissolution of a civil partnership.

Does living apart mean living in separate premises?
This is a very interesting point. There is no clear definition of "living apart". Living apart does not necessarily mean living in separate premises. Living apart is more a state of mind, rather than that of space. The intention is to show that both parties live independent lives regarding sleeping arrangements, holidays, meal times, caring for children, payment of bills, socialising and other arrangements. Living apart excludes one spouse working abroad or hospitalisation. The difficulty in relation to living apart is when does the clock "start", i.e. when officially has the couple commenced living apart? In the current economic

climate many separated couples (by agreement, judicial separation or dissolution of registered civil partnerships) may continue to live together under the same roof as there is no economic prospect or provision of finances to support separate premises.

Are family law cases heard in public? What protection do I have regarding my private matters?

Family law cases are held "in camera". This means all cases are held behind closed doors and only the relevant parties can attend. Until recently, general information regarding cases was unknown, but since recent amendments reporting now takes place regarding such cases at a general level, i.e. no specifics. The Courts Bill proposes to facilitate the updating of the law to allow reporting, subject to certain conditions, of family and child care proceedings. There is no indication as yet as to when this Bill will be published.

Maintenance Payments

What factors are taken into consideration when assessing maintenance payments?

In general the court decides what maintenance is proper. It takes into consideration the following factors (under section 5(4) of the Family Law (Maintenance of Spouses and Children) Act 1976):

- Income, earning capacity, property and other financial resources of the spouses and dependent children (and/ or other children)
- Financial responsibilities of each spouse
- Conduct of each spouse

Similarly, under the Civil Partnership and Certain Rights and Obligations of Cohabitants Act 2010 (Part 5, section 45) similar considerations are taken into account for the civil partner. Section 173(3) of the Act considers similar factors for both dependent qualified cohabitants and their former cohabitees.

In general, it is a combination of the best interests of the children and the needs and resources of each spouse, civil partner or former cohabitee. Therefore, the burden of financial restrictions must be shared between both parties. The standard of living before separation will not be same after separation.

The court must assess the minimum requirements of the dependent spouse, civil partner or former cohabitee and children, the net income of the maintenance-paying spouse, civil partner or cohabitee and the minimum living requirements of the maintenance-paying spouse, civil partner or cohabitee.

I have a child from a new relationship. Will this be taken into consideration?
In most cases, yes. Factors outside the marriage/civil partnership concerning children or other (new) partners can be and have been taken into consideration in the past.

Can maintenance orders be reviewed over time if there is a change in circumstances?
Yes, maintenance orders can be reviewed over time, dependent on circumstances changing, e.g. a dependent child becoming an adult, and/or changes in the financial circumstances of either party (maintenance-paying or maintenance-receiving spouse, civil partner or former cohabitee). It would be advisable to ensure a variation

order is included in the maintenance agreement (specifically for the maintenance payer), as non-inclusion will not allow the reduction in payment if required (under section 6 of the Family Law (Maintenance of Spouses and Children) Act 1976). Section 46 (registered civil partners) and section 183 (former cohabitees) of the Civil Partnership and Certain Rights and Obligations of Cohabitants Act 2010 allow for variation orders.

Maintenance payments have not been paid. What can I do?

Under sections 9 and 10 of the Family Law (Maintenance of Spouses and Children) Act 1976 (as amended by the Family Law Act 1995), previously maintenance payments were enforced through the courts and fines and/or imprisonment were imposed for breaches of payment. This has changed since the passing of the Civil Law (Miscellaneous Provisions) Act 2011. In some cases, deductions may be made from the maintenance payer's wage or salary. As we saw from Chapter 3, there has been reform of previous legislation that imposed a summons or warrant for the debtor's arrest and possible imprisonment for a maximum of three months as previously legislated under section 8 of the Enforcement of Court Orders Act 1940, as amended by section 22 of the Family Law Act 1995.

Legislation has now been amended with the passing of the Civil Law (Miscellaneous Provisions) Act 2011; section 31 of that Act imposes a newly revised process of fairness and transparency to seek a review of maintenance payments, but if breached can still result in sanctions by a judge.

In addition, the proposed Fines (Amendment) Bill, which is expected to be published in 2013, intends to provide for attachment of earnings and social welfare payments as an alternative to imprisonment for people who refuse to pay.

Under the Civil Partnership and Certain Rights and Obligations of Cohabitants Act 2010, section 53 may implement an attachment of earnings order for civil partners and section 176 similarly for former cohabiting couples.

I am concerned my former spouse will move to another country. Will the maintenance order still apply?

Yes, under numerous Acts; the Maintenance Order Act 1974 (for UK claims) can be administered in the District Court.

The Jurisdiction of Courts and Enforcement of Judgment (Amendment) Act 2012 and the Maintenance Act 1994 allows for maintenance orders to be enforced in other countries subject to those countries' jurisdictions. For enforcement of EU and international orders (excluding the UK) it is advisable to contact the Central Authority for Maintenance Recovery in the Department of Justice and Equality (mainrecov@justice.ie or 1890 555 509). Court maintenance agreements heard in one jurisdiction within the EU can be enforced across other EU states under EU legislation by court order with the assistance of the Central Authority for Maintenance Recovery. European enforcement orders, which are uncontested orders in operation since October 1995, can be enforced in other EU states without a need for court intervention. The International Recovery of Child Support (Hague Convention) Bill proposes to implement the Hague Convention on International Recovery of Child Support and other forms of family maintenance. This will further enhance and support the implementation of international maintenance orders and agreements. The Bill is expected to be published in 2013.

Judicial Separation

What is the difference between divorce and judicial separation?
Divorce is essentially a "no fault" decree allowing parties to remarry thereafter if the parties are in compliance with the eligibility criteria (four-year rule – see section on divorce) and accept the decree outcomes. A judicial separation is a separation agreement by the courts on a "fault" ground with the power to specify adjustment orders, i.e. orders through the lifetime of the parties. Both parties are still legally spouses after the completion of judicial separation, and therefore may still be entitled to access future assets, windfalls or inheritances of the other spouse during their lifetimes. Some spouses may not institute divorce on personal or religious grounds, or on grounds of reassessing the existing financial or ancillary arrangements.

Under the Civil Partnership and Certain Rights and Obligations of Cohabitants Act 2010, Part 12, section 110, essentially civil partners may only seek the dissolution of the partnership (similar to divorce) through the courts – and if granted can either register a new civil partnership or marry – or nullity of the registered civil partnership, i.e. state the registration was never valid from its inception and it was therefore an invalid civil partnership (discussed below). Dissolutions may be granted if the civil partners have lived apart from one another for a period of two years in the previous three years, and the court considers proper provision has been made for the civil partners. As civil partnerships only commenced in 2011, the first dissolutions may only commence in 2013 at the earliest.

So, what are the grounds for judicial separation?
The key grounds for availing of a judicial separation (section 2 of the Judicial Separation and Family Law Reform Act 1989) are:

* Adultery
* Inappropriate behaviour – this may be explained as unacceptable behaviour by one spouse. Such conduct may include mental or physical abuse and cruelty.
* Desertion – this must be for a period of at least one year (prior to court proceedings) and may include being forced to live away from the other spouse by just cause.
* Spouses have lived apart for at least three years (prior to commencing the application). This is required if both parties do not agree to proceedings. The period of time must be continuous.
* Spouses have lived apart for at least one year (prior to the court hearing). This is required if both parties agree to proceedings. The period of time must be continuous.
* No 'normal' relationship existed between the parties for at least one year (prior to date of application). This essentially means that there is a fundamental breakdown in the marriage relationship.

What factors must the court take into consideration in deciding the outcome of the separation?
The court must ensure that provision has been made for the dependent spouse and the welfare of dependent children (maximum maintenance rate per child is €150 per week and €500 per week for a spouse – District Court). Under

the Civil Partnership and Certain Rights and Obligations of Cohabitants Act 2010 hearings for the dissolution of a civil partnership will only take place in the Circuit Court, and there are no set minimum rates imposed.

What factors are taken into consideration in assessing such provisions?
Section 20(2) of the Judicial Separation and Family Law Reform Act 1989 identifies the key areas for assessment (for both parties, present and future) as:

* Income, earning capacity, property and other financial resources
* Financial needs, obligations and responsibilities of both parties
* Standard of living enjoyed by the family before proceedings

Under the Civil Partnership and Certain Rights and Obligations of Cohabitants Act 2010, section 129 considers the same key factors for the dissolution of civil partnerships and section 173 also considers the same assessable factors for separating former cohabitants.

What if one party still believes there is a possibility of reconciliation?
Proceedings would be suspended until the opportunity for reconciliation is investigated and exhausted. If this is not feasible, both parties, after a reasonable time, may return to recommence court proceedings (section 7(1) of the Judicial Separation and Family Law Reform Act 1989).

Under the Civil Partnership and Certain Rights and Obligations of Cohabitants Act 2010, section 111 may allow for the adjournment of proceedings for mediation to either reconcile or reach an agreement on the terms of the proposed dissolution. Section 193 also allows this provision for separating cohabiting couples. The option of mediation is not a compulsory requirement for either separating civil partnership or cohabiting couples.

Are the courts or legal bodies under any obligation to inform the parties of alternative dispute resolution methods or options for reconciliation before proceeding with judicial separation?
Yes. Under section 5 of the Judicial Separation and Family Law Reform Act 1989, legal representatives acting on behalf of each party shall ensure the person is informed of the following options:

- Marriage counselling (name and address of a potential counsellor should be provided)
- Family mediation (name and address of a potential mediator should be provided)
- Separation agreement

Legal representatives acting on behalf of their clients must present to the court a document signed by the parties clearly stating that they have been informed of the alternative options outlined above.

Nullity

What is an annulment and how can it be achieved?
An annulment is a judicial and/or an ecclesiastical pronouncement declaring a marriage invalid. To declare a marriage invalid, you must try to prove that a vital

element was not present at the time of marriage and therefore the marriage was null and void from the start. Prior to the Family Law (Divorce) Act 1996, annulment was essentially the only option available for people to legally remarry. Two kinds of annulment exist: a Church annulment (gives you the right to remarry within the Church) and a State annulment (your right to remarry is recognised by the State).

What is the difference between divorce and annulment?

An annulment is essentially the declaration that the marriage never existed at the time of inception (time of marriage) and therefore removes the obligation of ancillary orders, i.e. maintenance, etc. Divorce is the dissolution of marriage at the end of the relationship and may incur financial and other obligations for spouses and dependent children.

What are the key criteria for grounds for an annulment?

There are key criteria essential to the validity of marriage and these factors are used in determining if a marriage is void or voidable. The key grounds on which a marriage may be found to be void are:

- Non-observance of formalities – section 32 of the Family Law Act 1995 requires at least three months' notice be given in writing to the registrar in the relevant district of an intention to marry. Since 5 November 2007, under the Civil Registration Act 2004, both parties must go in person to the registrar.
- Lack of capacity – in this case, both parties must be free to join together in marriage, therefore neither party must be currently married, of the same sex, under

eighteen years of age (an exemption can be sought under section 33), or too closely related in degree of blood relationship.

- Lack of consent – both parties must give full, free and informed consent. Therefore a lack of consent may be found where there is:
  - ○ Mental incapacity (permanent or temporary), i.e. inability to understand the commitment
  - ○ Intoxication at the time of consent
  - ○ Fraud, mistake or misrepresentation, i.e. hiding of vital factors that may affect the decision to commit to marriage. Examples may include homosexuality or false character (presenting yourself as one type of person, but actually being another).
  - ○ Limited-purpose marriage, i.e. marrying for non-legitimate reasons (e.g. tax concessions, citizenship)
  - ○ Duress and undue influence, i.e. if a person's choice was threatened so much (physically, mentally or through life events) as to limit their ability to make a clear and free decision to marry.

There can also be voidable grounds. Voidable grounds are generally more personal and specific to the circumstances of the case. The voidable grounds are:

- Impotence – this may include physical or psychological factors affecting consummation of marriage up to and including the court submission. Impotence in this case excludes the ability to conceive.
- Inability to maintain a normal marital relationship – such an inability must be found to be present prior to marriage. Such factors may be the inability to maintain a marriage on psychiatric or immaturity grounds.

The burden of proof in all cases lies with the applicant on grounds of the balance of probabilities.

Under the Civil Partnership and Certain Rights and Obligations of Cohabitants Act 2010, section 107, civil partners may seek nullity on the grounds of breach of the fundamental requirements:

- Age
- One or both partners was already married or in a civil partnership
- The formalities of notification and compliance were not observed
- One or both parties did not give informed consent or they were under duress
- One or both partners was not of the right mind to understand the commitment
- The partners were within the prohibited degree of relationship
- The partners were not of the same sex and therefore were ineligible to register a civil partnership

Divorce

What factors are taken into consideration in assessing the outcome of divorce?
Section 20(2) of the Family Law (Divorce) Act 1996 clearly identifies the key areas for assessment (both parties, present and future) as:

- Income, earning capacity, property and other financial resources
- Financial needs, obligations and responsibilities
- Standard of living enjoyed by the family before proceedings

- Age of each spouse, duration of marriage and length of time living together (pre-marriage)
- Physical and mental disability of either spouse
- Contributions made by each party (financial or homemaker)
- Earning capacity of each party (to adapt to future changes)
- Conduct of each party
- Accommodation needs of each spouse
- Terms of a separation agreement (if entered into by the parties), if still in place

Dissolution of a civil partnership (Part 12 of the Civil Partnership and Certain Rights and Obligations of Cohabitants Act 2010) is similar to a decree of divorce allowing the right to register a new civil partnership or marriage and break succession rights, although section 127 of the Act allows a former civil partner, within six months of the granting of representation (see Chapter 3 – Wills and Inheritance) of his or her deceased civil partner, to submit an application to the Court to state proper provision was not made to the surviving civil partner during the lifetime of the deceased. It is not possible for the surviving civil partner to apply if they have registered a new civil partnership or have married since the dissolution.

Under section 194 of the Civil Partnership and Certain Rights and Obligations of Cohabitants Act 2010 a former cohabitant can also apply within six months of the granting of representation for provision from the deceased cohabitant's estate, but only if the relationship ended less than two years prior to the death of the deceased. The applicant can apply if the relationship ended more than two years prior to the death, but only if the surviving former cohabitant was in receipt of payment from the deceased former cohabitant or if proceedings were pending at the time of death. The court will need to assess the financial dependency of the surviving former cohabitant. In addition, the former surviving cohabitant cannot apply if they have since married or registered a civil partnership.

What are the eligibility requirements for obtaining a divorce?

As per section 5(1) of the Family Law (Divorce) Act 1996, the criteria are:

- The spouses have lived apart from each other for four of the previous five years.
- There is no reasonable prospect of reconciliation between spouses.
- Such provisions (financial, custody and/or access) as the court considers proper in the best interests of the parties and dependent members of the family (children aged up to 18 years, children under 23 in full-time education and/or suffering mental or physical disability) exist or will be made.

If all of the above have been complied with the court may grant a decree of divorce in respect of the marriage concerned.

For the dissolution of a civil partnership, section 110(*a*) of the Civil Partnership and Certain Rights and Obligations of Cohabitants Act 2010 states that civil partners must have lived apart for two years during the previous three years. The court will then grant a dissolution of the civil partnership if, under section 110(*b*), it is satisfied that "provision that the court considers proper having regard to the circumstances exist or will be made for the civil partner".

Are the courts or legal bodies under any obligation to inform the parties of alternative dispute resolution methods or options for reconciliation before proceeding with divorce?

Yes. Under section 6 of the Family Law (Divorce) Act 1996 legal representatives acting on behalf of each party shall ensure the person is informed of the following options:

- Marriage counselling (name and address of a potential counsellor should be provided)
- Family mediation (name and address of a potential mediator should be provided)
- Separation agreement, either mutually or by a court order (judicial separation)

Legal representatives acting on behalf of their clients must present to the court a document signed by the parties clearly stating they have been informed of the alternative options stated above.

What if one party still believes there is a possibility of reconciliation?

Proceedings would be suspended until the opportunity for reconciliation is investigated and exhausted. If reconciliation is found to not be feasible, both parties, after a reasonable time, may return to recommence court proceedings (section 8(1)).

We feel we can sort all issues regarding our divorce (personal and legal) ourselves before bringing the matter to court. Is this possible?

No. Under section 9, no written communication between the parties to seek reconciliation or agreement on all or

.part of the issues shall be admissible as evidence in court. Therefore the judge may override any prior agreements (other than separation agreements in place) in independently assessing the proper needs of all the parties.

Can I carry out a "do-it-yourself" divorce?

Yes, you may be able to carry out the administration of your divorce yourself, subject to no complex proceedings, i.e. no proceedings related to property or maintenance, etc. As part of the divorce proceedings, certain documentation must be complied with (and signed by a practising solicitor or barrister or practising commissioner of oaths). It is always advisable to seek independent legal opinion in more complex cases before proceeding.

Is divorce a "full and final settlement"?

No. With reference to maintenance, payments may be made in either a lump sum or by instalments or periodic payments after the divorce (section 13). Pension adjustment orders may also be made for the purpose of pension payments (section 17). In relation to divorce, a spouse will always be classified as a spouse for the purpose of maintenance.

A spouse, even after divorce, may return to the court to seek a maintenance review order (section 15). Such maintenance orders may cease on grounds of remarriage of the receiving spouse (section 13(5)). Even after the death of a spouse, the surviving spouse may be eligible to seek an order of such provision from the estate if they were not adequately provided for during their lifetime as a spouse (section 18(1)). This may not be achievable if the surviving spouse has remarried (section 18(2)).

Does divorce remove the legal right share of inheritance?
Yes, generally the legal right share of your former spouse
is fully extinguished on the completion of a divorce
(excluding above). Therefore the former spouse is no
longer a spouse for inheritance purposes.

*Is there such a thing as a "quickie" divorce? And what are
the rules?*
A "quickie" divorce may exist under what is known as the
Brussels II Convention. The Brussels II Convention may
also be applicable in other cases including annulment and
separation. EU law supersedes Irish law, so therefore a
divorce under the Brussels II Convention may be applicable after twelve months, subject to certain criteria. This
supersedes the existing Irish divorce law, which states
that the parties must be living apart for four of the preceding five years.

The criteria for a divorce under the Brussels II
Convention include the stipulation that one of the parties must be domiciled or habitually resident in another
jurisdiction of the EU, excluding Denmark, for a period of
one year (article 2). Jurisdictions in the United Kingdom
are defined as individual legal systems, i.e. England,
Scotland, Wales and Northern Ireland. The jurisdiction
where the relevant papers are first submitted is generally where the case will be heard (article 11(1)). In these
cases, judgments given in the courts of first instance (first
received) will be recognised in all others. The European
Court of Justice has ruled that spouses holding the same
dual nationality in the EU may choose to institute divorce
proceedings before the courts of either of the two member
states concerned.

So what is "domiciled" or "habitually resident" defined as?

To be described as being "domiciled" in a particular country, that country is generally defined as your country of origin or the country with which you are most profoundly associated, i.e. the country where you choose to live, have resided in or that has become your "home". "Habitually resident" is a little more difficult to define. You are generally referred to as being habitually resident in a country when you have resided in that country for over one year and you can show a pattern of living in or presence there.

Civil Legal Aid and Legal Advice

How can you qualify for civil legal aid? Is it means tested?

Civil legal aid is a means-tested assistance for representation by a solicitor (and barrister, if necessary). The threshold for eligibility is €18,000 disposable income per annum and disposable capital of €320,000 (i.e. premises or valuables). Disposable income is total income (social welfare, employment, self-employment and other sources) less income tax, PRSI, accommodation costs (rent or mortgage repayments up to a maximum of €8,000 per year), childcare (up to a maximum of €6,000 per child) and possible other expenses. In addition, there is an allowable deduction of €3,500 for a spouse/partner (if they are dependent on you) and €1,600 for each dependent child (under 18 or over 18 in full-time education and dependant on you).

The minimum fee payable is €50 (subject to a means test and disposable income of less than €11,500 or if you are on social welfare payments only). The rate increases by a further 25 per cent on the excess of disposable income above €11,500. Capital is also assessed (and converted as a percentage to a contribution rate depending on the amount). Extreme hardship cases will be assessed on their own merits. Legal advice through civil legal aid can be provided through verbal or written advice. A minimum fee of €10 must be paid for legal advice through this channel. For further details please check www.legalaidboard. ie, or contact the Legal Aid Board at 066-9471000.

Legal aid is provided specifically in the following areas:

- Judicial separation
- Divorce
- Maintenance
- Domestic violence
- Custody of or access to children
- Hire purchase agreements, landlord–tenant disputes (excluding land) and contract disputes

Criminal legal aid is provided free of charge (subject to a means test and approval by the judge). Free legal advice may also be available through Free Legal Advice Centres (FLAC) around the country. Such centres are, in the majority, run in conjunction with the Citizens Information Centres. FLAC presents an opportunity for individuals to gain some legal opinion or direction. This service does not provide any one-to-one representation for clients and is not to be mistaken for civil legal aid or legal advice from the Legal Aid Board.

What if I am entitled to legal aid in Ireland, but the case of first instance is in another EU country? How will costs be assessed?
If you are eligible for civil legal aid in your "home" country, a certificate of approval will be required to be

presented in the court of first instance to allow you to benefit from legal aid in that jurisdiction (article 31 of the Brussels II Convention).

Sale of the Family Home

What powers do the courts have in relation to the "family home"?

First, let us define the "family home". The family home (under the Family Home Protection Act 1976) is defined as "primarily a dwelling in which a married couple ordinarily reside. The expression comprises, in addition, a dwelling in which a spouse whose protection is in issue ordinarily resides or, if that spouse has left the other spouse, ordinarily resided before so leaving." The courts, via property adjustment orders, may:

- Transfer property between parties
- Force the sale and division of property
- Alter a previous separation agreement regarding property
- Reduce either party's stake in a property

Property adjustment orders may also include other assets including stocks, shares, holiday homes and all other valuable (commercially sellable) items.

Other orders (e.g. Miscellaneous Ancillary Orders) may also provide a right to reside for a fixed period of time.

Under the Civil Partnership and Certain Rights and Obligations of Cohabitants Act 2010, section 118 allows for the provision of property adjustment orders for registered civil partners and section 128 may order the sale of property. Section 174 of the Act also allows for the provision of property adjustment orders for former cohabiting couples. Section 27 of the Act defines a "shared home" as a dwelling in which civil partners ordinarily reside.

Can my husband sell the family home without my consent?
No. Under the Family Home Protection Act 1976, the consent of the spouse is required. This even occurs in cases where the spouse has no financial or legal ownership of the home. Such consent must be in writing and have been agreed before the sale. The family home is defined (section 2) as the dwelling in which a married couple ordinarily reside.

However, since the introduction of the Family Law Act 1995, "open-ended" consent may be given by the spouse for any future sales. It is essential to ensure consent is voluntary, informed (you have an understanding of what is being signed) and is given without undue influence, duress or misrepresentation.

Are there any exceptions to the rule?
Yes, there are some exceptions (section 4). These are as follows:

- Desertion
- Unsound mind or mental disability
- Spouse cannot be found
- Unreasonable to withhold consent

Sections 29–33 of the Civil Partnership and Certain Rights and Obligations of Cohabitants Act 2010 prevent a civil partner from selling, mortgaging, leasing or transferring the shared home (known as "conveyance") without the consent of the other civil partner. The courts have the power to control consent if it considers it unreasonable for the civil partner to withhold consent, taking into account a number of factors, which may include the needs and resources of the civil partners. These factors may include the mental health of the civil partners (within the meaning of the Mental Health Act 2001), consideration of an offer of suitable and alternative accommodation, or if the civil partner cannot be found (section 29). A civil partner is also able to apply to the courts for orders restraining the other civil partner from doing anything that might reduce his or her interest in the shared home or make it unsuitable to live in (section 30).